1917 -

Photocopy

£2
5-

FURTHER EDUCATION

AND

DEMOCRACY

by

Keith Wymer

Bilston College Publications
in association with
Education Now

First published 1996 by Bilston Community College Publications in association with Education Now Books.

Bilston College Publications, Bilston (EO & C) Training Ltd., Bilston Community College, Green Lanes, Wellington Road, Bilston, Wolverhampton, WV14 6EW, England.

Education Now Publishing Co-operative Ltd, PO Box 186, Derby

British Library Cataloguing in Publication Data
A catalogue record for this book is available from the British Library

ISBN 1-871526-26-4

Design and production: Bilston College Publications in association with the Education Now Publishing Co-operative Ltd.

Printed by Mastaprint, Sandiacre, Nottinghamshire.

CONTENTS

Foreword

Acknowledgements

Preface

1 Introduction: The birth of the further education sector   1

   Further education and politics
   The further education voice
   Quangocracy and competition

2 Chapter One: Flight to incorporation   8

   Further education in the 1980s
   The white paper *Education and Training* for the 21st
   Century and the 1992 Further and Higher Education Act
   Issues resolved and unresolved

3 Chapter Two: Corporations and their minders   21

   Corporations and the Department for Education (DfE)
   Corporations and the Further Education Funding
   Council (FEFC)
   Corporations and chief executives (principals)

4 Chapter Three: Community colleges and educating the   38
                   community

   The evolution of community colleges
   The need for community education
   The community education alternative

5   Chapter Four: Equal opportunities and quangocracy   49

         Equal opportunities and community education
         Equal opportunities and quangocracy
         Equal opportunities through community education:
         the FEFC's response

6   Chapter Five: Community College Strategy and Management: 59
                         The Bilston Consortium

         Community colleges before 1984
         Bilston Community College
         The Bilston Consortium: development of the community
         college concept

7   Chapter Six: The international challenge and economic   77
                        re-generation

         India in Bilston and Bilston in Moscow
         The United Kingdom and Western Europe
         Community colleges and economic re-generation

8   Chapter Seven: Education, training and the economy   90

         Economic policy and employment
         The reform of post-16 education
         Resourcing a comprehensive system

9   Chapter Eight: Further education and democracy   105

         Democracy and internationalism: South Africa
         Democracy and community colleges

         Abbreviations and acronyms   111

         References and bibliography   113

         Index   116

Dedication

To Nelson Mandela

The most inspirational democrat of our time.

Foreword
by Dennis Turner MP
Chairman of the All Party Group for Further Education

Keith Wymer's new book *Further Education and Democracy* represents a powerful critique of government policies on education and employment, market forces, Europe and the World Economy. He demonstrates very forcibly the failure of our further education system, shackled by a lack of identity and integration and by narrow vocationalism, to positively respond to the real education, economic and employment needs of our local communities which colleges want to serve.

I have known Keith Wymer for 30 years in which time I have come to admire and appreciate his simple philosophy, his strong leadership and a sincerity of purpose. Time and again he has overcome the obstacles and adversities which sought to frustrate the accomplishment of his vision of a real community-based college genuinely meeting all of the education needs of local people.

Bilston has grown from a college of 5,000 students at the time it was created in 1984 by Wolverhampton's Labour Council, to an institution of over 40,000 students now. I am proud to have been associated with the college as Chairman of the Further Education Committee when it was established and more recently as a member of the college's corporation.

Since entering parliament in 1987, when I, together with Alun Michael, Ken Hargreaves and David Clelland, established the first Parliamentary All Party Group for Further Education, I have observed Keith gain a well deserved regional, national and international reputation for his boundless energy and commitment to further education.

I hope all those concerned for the success of Britain and the education and progress of its citizens will read this book. It is clear in the light of our recent history that there is a desperate need for fundamental, social, political, as well as educational changes. This book demonstrates that further education locally accountable and democratically controlled can play a leading part in the renewal and revitalisation of our community spirit and enterprise, at the same time as playing a critical part in the economic re-generation of the country.

the cause alone is worthy, the next day brings the best

William Morris.

Acknowledgements

The belief that democracy can be restored to further education, the reason this book has been written, has been kept alive by commitment to the democratic cause of Bilston Community College governors to the democratic cause. Although reasons for optimism on this count are not easy to find in England (beyond the ex members of the Further Education Campaign Group), the positiveness of colleagues in the USA and South Africa has been a great encouragement.

Professor Eric Robinson has been generous, as ever, in allowing me to use his material, Alan Millington and Dennis Turner (chair and vice chair of the corporation) reached the point where they could not buy me a drink without a reminder, and Frank Reeves (our editor) despaired by issuing deadlines.

The writing is the easy and enjoyable bit - at least for me if not for my tolerant family. Rita and Mary of my office have been tireless in searching for reference material, even when they have been convinced (occasionally correctly) that I have it at home.

The short straw fell (she didn't draw it) to Verolyn, a genius on the word processor, and Ian Kenny who delayed his holiday to complete the index.

It has been a genuine team effort, as befits a book on participation and democracy. The contribution of my closest colleagues - Jenny, Sara, Sim, Paul and Frank - has been in sustaining the belief that working in further education is worthwhile.

Nevertheless, the responsibility for any failures and limitations, and for the views expressed, is entirely mine. Further education is a large subject and I am acutely aware that the attempt to cover so many facets means that some are addressed inadequately. Democracy is an even larger subject and the treatment even more inadequate.

There are no easy answers but if the result of this book is that the questions are debated more seriously, its objective will have been achieved.

Preface

From the time (1991) the white paper *Education and Training for the 21st Century* was published, Bilston Community College governors and management persistently opposed the proposals for the 1992 Further and Higher Education Act. This seemed odd to colleagues who knew that the college had been locked in battle with Wolverhampton Local Education Authority (LEA) for several years. In common with many parts of the country, the conflict was over funding, interference in management and disregard of governors' powers.

The Act was opposed because, at a stroke, it swept away all traces of democracy and established a plethora of quangos called corporations, operating under a super-duper quango: the Further Education Funding Council (FEFC), (throughout, reference is made only to the Further Education Funding Council of England). It also accentuated divisions (academic and vocational, vocational and non- vocational, school sixth forms and colleges, education and training) when the pressing need was to remove them. One reason the Act failed to tackle the main problems was that the Department for Education (DfE) knew very little about further education colleges: the information collected nationally from LEAs was inadequate and largely out-of-date. All the early decisions of the FEFC were inspired guesses unsupported by hard evidence: it was fortunate for colleges that some of the guesses were rather good.

Given the sorry state of further education in 1996, it is small comfort to be proved right in opposing the 1992 Act. In *The Modernity of Further Education* (1995), Frank Reeves has already demonstrated the potential damage of quangocracy. *Further Education and Democracy* is an eleventh hour attempt to argue that all need not be lost. But lost all will be if government is not persuaded to remove the divisions ignored in 1992; to adopt a broader, lifelong-learning (rather than narrow vocational) approach to curriculum; to fund expansion at a reasonable level.

This book will draw on the Bilston experience, on the grounds that the community approach to education is the only means of increasing participation to the level necessary to meet national education and training targets. It will also show that other countries regard democratically accountable community colleges as the most effective means of extending access. If there is a lack of modesty in proposals for change, the justification is that positive statements on behalf of further education are the best means of creating a constructive debate - to draw attention to the value of colleges to society in general and to the economy in particular.

Democracy in further education is a complex concept. The removal of local councillors from governing bodies in 1992 would have been of limited significance had it not occurred as one of a number of government measures to curb local participation. Although the principled position will not be ignored, this book will concentrate on examining democracy, or the lack of it, in the practice of further education. It will attempt to demonstrate that the democratic approach can ensure a more relevant and better quality service for students and communities, as well as a more effective use of scarce resources.

The way forward, it will be argued, is to escape from the narrow vocationalism of the government's education and training policies. A first step is to persuade the United Kingdom government to adopt a more positive attitude to the education and training position of the European Parliament, with its emphasis on lifelong learning and concern for excluded people, especially the unemployed. This is not a matter of replacing a national with a super-national context but a plea for recognition of the value and relevance of a commitment to internationalism.

A unified and democratic system at sixteen plus obviously requires legislation. Meanwhile, corporations should use their independence to maximise community and college participation in governance and management. Paradoxically, the ability of corporations to meet the education and training needs of their local communities depends on how far they are prepared to use their independence to form partnerships - at home and internationally.

Introduction:

The birth of the further education sector

Further education and politics

Granting independence to further education and sixth form colleges was consistent with the government's policy of reducing the influence of local authorities. Establishing corporations to compete with one another, and with schools, was equally consistent with the free market economy philosophy of increasing efficiency through competition.   In addition, the failure of Department-of-Employment-supported training schemes to improve in any significant way the skills available to employers meant that something had to be done to give national targets for education and training a degree of credibility.

For the majority of politicians and civil servants, further education colleges have some sort of vague role in the grey area between schools and universities. The lack of government knowledge is nowhere more evident than the information available in other countries about United Kingdom education and training, the responsibility of agencies such as the British Council, the Overseas Development Administration, individual civil servants in, for example, Brussels. European Commission circulars inviting applications for project funding rarely mention further education: when this is pointed out, the response is that colleges can apply as either schools or universities.

When he introduced the white paper, *Education and Training for the 21st Century*, Kenneth Clarke, Secretary of State for Education, knew very little about further education and he was equally ill-informed about non-vocational classes. In private conversation he differed from many politicians by fully recognising his ignorance: his response to difficult questions was that corporations would be free to sort out the problems. Clarke was, nevertheless, interested enough to argue at length over a pint, whereas John Patten, his successor, left a meeting of principals and governors after ten minutes, stating that, as his knowledge of further education was limited, his junior ministers and civil servants would deal with the issues raised.

2 The birth of the further education sector

The only stroke of luck during the first two years of incorporation was the appointment of the two ministers responsible for further education. Nigel Forman retired after a few months, officially through ill-health but there were suspicions that he was not treated well by his boss. His sincerity and commitment were not in doubt and he made every effort to meet, and listen to, representatives of the further education sector. He recognised the necessity to address a number of questions left in the air by the 1992 Further and Higher Education Act, notably the uncertain position of adult education, which remained the responsibility of local education authorities.

Tim Boswell proved to be an excellent minister and continued along the same lines as his predecessor. He took up the adult education issue, recognised the problems arising from the division between education and training, and did not share John Patten's enthusiasm for creating new sixth forms. Even more encouraging, he was not in sympathy with the aggressive approach to the trade unions of the Colleges' Employers' Forum (CEF). Tim worked tirelessly on behalf of further education and his transfer to another government department in 1995 ended any illusion that the value of further education was recognised by the Major government. The Prime Minister's interest - he appeared alongside John Patten to address principals and corporation chairs early in 1993 - was short-lived.

Kenneth Clarke launched further education as an independent sector in 1992 and introduced the three-year public expenditure settlement which confirmed that it would suffer severe cuts in November 1995. In between there had been rapid growth of student numbers, and efficiency gains of almost 20 per cent. Although few in the service would deny the necessity to improve efficiency 1993/96, the budget requirement for a further 20 per cent 1996/99 was beyond the reasonable expectation of anyone aware of the needs of the service and of the large number of people denied access to education and training. The budget treatment confirmed that, unlike schools and universities, further education colleges carry no political weight: the conventional wisdom is that there are no votes in it. The response to a letter sent to 60 MPs on further education funding in October 1995 was five replies and seven acknowledgements.

The Labour Party, in the form of Jack Straw, Shadow Secretary of State for Education, aligned itself vaguely with the local authorities in opposition to the 1992 Further and Higher Education Act. From statements made at the time, it was not clear whether Jack Straw was for or against incorporation. Although the Shadow spokesperson for further education, Derek Fatchett, offered a much improved policy for unifying the academic and vocational curriculum, he was not committed to tackling the structural problems which prevented a unifying approach - the divisions between school sixth forms and colleges, academic and vocational studies, education and training, vocational and non-vocational education. During the 1992 general election campaign it was uncertain whether a Labour government would implement the Act or repeal it.

The Labour Party position was no more convincing between 1993 and 1996. It was not even clear that the front bench welcomed the bringing together of further education and training in one department when the Department of Employment was abolished in 1995. David Blunkett (who succeeded Jack Straw), and Bryan Davies, who became the Shadow spokesperson for further education, both had experience of further education, and understood the issues, but it was not party policy to give it priority. When Tony Blair and Harriet Harman sent their children to, respectively, an opted out and selective school it became doubtful that the have nots of further education would be given priority by a Blair-led government. Although Gordon Brown, Shadow Chancellor, regarded training as key to his economic policies, he rarely mentioned further education.

The further education voice

When, in 1991, the government decided to legislate it did not know which groups to consult. Given the hostility resulting from persistent attacks on local government it was unlikely that much could be gained from talking to local education authorities. Civil servants arranged informal meetings with groups of principals around the country in a hurried attempt to find out about colleges. The Further Education Campaign Group (FECG), the Tertiary Colleges' Association (TCA), the Association of Colleges for Further and Higher Education (ACFHE), the Association of Principals of Colleges (APC), were all consulted by ministers but it is probable that the views expressed resulted in an even greater state of muddle and confusion amongst ministers and civil servants. Because there was no reliable information about colleges and their students nationally, there was no firm factual base for the white paper *Education and Training for the 21st Century* and the 1992 Further and Higher Education Act. The DfE perception was that colleges recruited full-time from schools and day release from among young employees, plus a few unemployed funded by Training and Enterprise Councils (TECs). Ministers and officials were unaware of the large number of unemployed students supported by LEAs, often with European funding.

The absence of a single voice speaking on behalf of further education meant that the ministerial door was more open than is usual to groups with vested interests who wanted their views to be known. One such group was known as the Big Booming Five. The membership must remain anonymous to prevent the sector being regarded with even greater ridicule but the five were frequently to be observed leaving Whitehall or Westminster. There is no evidence that they had any influence, although they undoubtedly added to the general confusion about further education. One of the factors about the Big Booming Five was that, when national statistics became available as a result of the exertions of colleges and the FEFC, they were not as big as they thought they were, and the booming faded.

The closest regular links with politicians during the period leading up to incorporation were those between members of the All Party Committee of the House of Commons, (established in 1990 to lobby for tertiary education) and the Tertiary Colleges' Association and the Further Education Campaign Group. The All Party Committee for Tertiary Education was chaired by Dennis Turner, Labour, with two Conservatives, Ken Hargreaves and John Bovis, acting as secretaries 1990/94. After incorporation this Committee broadened its brief to the whole of further education, with links to colleges through the newly formed Association for Colleges (AfC).

The Association for Colleges was established as a result of a merger of the Tertiary Colleges' Association, the Further Education Campaign Group, the Association of Colleges for Further and Higher Education. The Association of Principals of Colleges and the Sixth Form Colleges' Association hovered on the margin but could not bring themselves to wind up their organisations and join the AfC. Its brief was to represent the further education sector on all matters except staff pay and conditions. Unfortunately, it got off to a slow start, partly because it took over a year to find a suitable chief executive.

The Colleges' Employers' Forum (CEF), set up as a complementary organisation to deal with pay and conditions, was much quicker off the mark. Roger Ward (roaring Roger) was appointed Chief Executive and immediately set about the National Association of Teachers in Further and Higher Education (NATFHE).   Most corporations recognised that incorporation meant that NATFHE could not continue to *manage* colleges by means of the Silver Book, an expensive LEA legacy on pay and conditions of service. They were less unanimous on the confrontational approach adopted by Roger, especially when no national agreement was reached and corporations were left to negotiate their own deals at local level.

The DfE handed over the running of the further education sector to the Further Education Funding Council (FEFC). Bill Stubbs (later Sir William) was appointed Chief Executive and tried to bring some order to the chaos. When he achieved a standstill budget for the first two years he was hailed as something of a miracle worker by principals who, under LEA control, had come to expect budget reductions every year. It is not necessary to agree with all their decisions to recognise that, without the strong leadership of Stubbs and McClure (Director of Finance) 1993/95, further education could have fallen into even greater chaos than under LEAs.

When corporations tried to exercise their freedom they discovered there was not a great deal of it. The pressures on colleges were considerable, especially the frequent audits as the FEFC attempted to collect reliable information, and from NATFHE industrial action when no national agreement was reached on new contracts. The victims were often chief executives who no longer had directors of education to defend them: over 100 departed 1992/96. In some cases, no doubt, they were not up to the job but their legal and professional position - in relation to corporations and the FEFC - was less than clear, and they were obvious scapegoats when things started to go wrong.

Quangocracy and competition

The 1992 Further and Higher Education Act swept away all remnants of democracy in further education. LEAs were replaced by corporations, theoretically responsible for strategy, and the FEFC, responsible for funding. Since many colleges relied almost entirely on the FEFC for funding, their freedom on strategy was severely restrained. The tension between the Act's intention to give corporations freedom and the FEFC's enthusiasm for regulations (far beyond funding) was one of the major problems, especially for colleges willing to take the initiative and expand.

In terms of its purpose - to improve, expand and make more efficient education and training at 16 plus - the 1992 Act did less than half a job. The failure to create a unified system, structurally and in terms of the curriculum, restricted

6   The birth of the further education sector

student opportunity and wasted resources.   John Patten made the situation worse by approving new sixth forms; TECs continued to be responsible for training; LEAs for non-vocational adult education.   Worse still, schools were given permission to offer courses to adults and, following the 1995 government white paper *Competitiveness: Forging Ahead,*   anybody could apply to the FEFC for funding for vocational education.   A unified system would have released at least as much funding as the cuts to college budgets 1996/99.

Although the three main political parties supported the rapid expansion of education and training at 16 plus,   only the Liberal Democrats openly recognised that more money is required.   Even if colleges are able to cope with cuts and continue to expand 1996/99, without significant additional funds (especially for buildings and equipment), national education and training targets cannot be met - and there is already recognition that, if the United Kingdom is to match competitors, the targets are too modest.

Where is the money coming from? is a question which must be addressed. *Full employment* could generate additional resources for the government, but since this will not occur without changes in economic policy which include more and higher quality education and training, especially for adults, increased taxation is the only option in the short term.   There is reason to believe that the electorate could be persuaded to accept this as a sounder investment than an escalating commitment to pay people to do nothing.

The chapters which follow will examine recent changes in further education, assess their relevance to education and training needs, and then attempt to chart the way forward.

Chapter One shows how vocationalism tightened its grip on colleges in the 1980s and how local education authorities proved incapable of providing the necessary resources and support.   Legislation was necessary but the 1992 Further and Higher Education Act failed to create a unified open access system, with equal opportunities for all.

Chapter Two describes the relationships between corporations and the Department for Education (DfE), latterly the Department for Education and Employment (DfEE); corporations and the Further Education Funding Council (FEFC); and the DfE/FEFC relationship during the first three years of incorporation.   It also considers the role of chief executives and college managers, operating uneasily in the context of inexperienced corporations and the FEFC.

Chapters Three and Four explain why the vocationalised further education curriculum will not meet the needs of the *other half*, who have previously been denied education and training after leaving school. The vocational emphasis is inimical to equal opportunities and community education.

Chapter Five uses the new (1996) organisation and management structure of Bilston Community College to illustrate the evolution of the community college concept. Community colleges developed in the USA in the 1950s and the community college ideal is now being adopted to provide adult education and training in Southern Africa and other developing nations.

Chapter Six attempts to show that in a rapidly shrinking world the context for education and training is international rather than national. It is argued that the resources issue can be addressed only by integrating education, training, economic development.

Chapter Seven outlines a legislative framework for post-16 education and training integrated with economic re-generation. The resources question is as much about efficient organisation and management of the curriculum as about new money.

Chapter Eight attempts to address the practical problems in operating democratically leaning heavily on the ideas of Professor Eric Robinson, formerly Director of Lancashire Polytechnic. It is argued that the campaign for democracy in further education has a much greater chance of success if it is internationalised.

Chapter One

Flight to incorporation

Further education in the 1980s

The 1944 Education Act envisaged a minimum of part-time education in colleges for all school-leavers. County colleges would offer education for 16-18 year olds released from work for up to two days a week. A Ministry of Education white paper, *Youth Opportunities* (1945), advocated a broad, general education, with subjects including art, drama and physical education. Although, without compulsory day release, it was never likely that a national system of county colleges would become a reality, it was important for the future of further education that a few pioneering principals (Fred Flower at Kingsway, Harry Lamb at Bilston) kept the concept alive for a generation. The sections of the Act which applied to further and adult education were never repealed, merely ignored, then forgotten, and finally made irrelevant by the 1988 Education Reform Act.

When day release expanded in the fifties and sixties it was more vocational than general, with employers the dominant influence. After the 1964 Industrial Training Act, which established industrial training boards, the Department of Employment (DE) became more influential than the Department of Education and Science (DES). A number of industries, notably engineering and construction, established strong training boards which, because of their financial clout, effectively took over whole departments in some colleges. The colleges where part-time day release grew most rapidly were more accurately described as *technical* rather than *further education* colleges.

While day release grew much more slowly than governments planned (HMSO, 1964), there was significant growth in full-timers. They came, mainly, from secondary modern schools, which had no sixth forms but offered GCE O levels and CSEs. Although there was strong competition when sixth forms were established by comprehensive schools, the number of full-timers in colleges continued to increase steadily throughout the seventies. Some comprehensive schools made genuine attempts to develop curriculum for all at 16 plus but GCE A levels dominated, with most vocational work in colleges. Effective co-ordination of school and college provision, attempted by some LEAs, was exceptional. Because status and funding was enhanced by large sixth forms, pupils, especially the achievers, were strongly encouraged to stay on at school.

Tertiary colleges, defined at the time as sole providers of education and training for full-time and part-time 16-18 year olds in a specified area, became increasingly popular after 1980, as did sixth-form colleges which provided for full-time students only. Because LEAs were responsible for the pattern of post-16 education within their boundaries, there were wide variations from area to area in opportunities and in encouragement for staying on beyond the school-leaving age. Because most of the early tertiary colleges were based on an amalgamation of school sixth forms, the majority of day students were under 18. The emphasis started to change when tertiary colleges were established in urban areas, based on existing further education colleges rather than on school sixth form amalgamation.

As further education expanded there was conflict with local authority education departments, which frequently continued to treat colleges as if they were schools. In an attempt to establish a degree of independence from education officers and councillors, in 1970 the DES modified instruments and articles of government (DES, 1970). One important change was to reduce LEA councillors to one third of the membership of governing bodies, with, typically, one third from the college and one third from the community (including employers and trade unions). Where LEAs accepted the spirit, as well as the letter, of the change colleges gained in terms of management control and in governor contribution to strategic development.

Unfortunately, in too many cases, education officers continued to try to manage colleges from education departments. Also, because some LEAs determined budgets without consultation with governors (despite article of government stipulation to the contrary), they were in a position to frustrate development plans. Where there were sixth forms, it was frequently LEA policy that most full-time study should be in schools, with colleges concentrating on courses for part-time students and full-time study only in specified vocational curriculum areas. Competition was inevitable, especially in the GCE A level sphere, with small classes in colleges and sixth forms. A headteacher's reference to *night school in the day* was not an untypical perception of colleges.

The government's funding of further education in resource allocations to LEAs was based on the assumption that students were either full-time, or part-time day release, with the majority 16-18. The reality by the 1980s was that the majority were over 18, with the participation rate of unemployed adults rising year by year. The DES funded LEAs on the basis of the further education statistical return (FESR), which largely ignored students who were unemployed. Some LEAs did not pass on to colleges all the funding they received, while others funded students who were unemployed from their own resources (or from funding acquired from Europe such as the European Social Fund). An inevitable consequence was widely varying levels of funding, with some colleges receiving twice as much as others per full-time student equivalent.

The influence of the Department of Employment, which strengthened with the setting up of industrial training boards after the 1964 Industrial Training Act, continued to increase. As unemployment rose, money for youth and adult training schemes was channelled through the Department of Employment rather than the DES and LEAs. Local authorities' influence continued to the extent that training was offered in colleges, and because they are major employers, but there was an increasing government preference for private sector training, where possible without day release to colleges. Even where private training agencies offered quality vocational training, they struggled to provide the basic skills support needed by many students.

By the time the Manpower Services Commission (MSC) was set up in January 1974 local government influence in training was marginal. The MSC was a quango operating on a national basis, without any democratic accountability. It had very limited success, principally because its brief was based on a misunderstanding of the problems to be addressed. The training for employees was generally too narrowly vocational to meet the needs of the economy for a more flexible workforce: when applied to the unemployed (whose greatest needs were literacy, numeracy, basic social skills) it was largely irrelevant. Instead of offering jobless teenagers and adults further education courses of their choice, they were offered short term projects, rarely leading to recognised qualifications.   Because the assumption was that economic upturn was just around the corner, the purpose was to keep people out of the unemployment statistics rather than assist them to acquire qualifications.

Those colleges concerned primarily with part-time students became heavily dependent on the MSC for income. In many instances they continued to offer narrow vocationalism: unemployed students were enrolled with MSC support not only to obtain income for colleges, but also to fill unused facilities and staff timetables. For example, in areas where engineering was in decline, with poor employment prospects, unemployed people were given traditional engineering training because there were unused engineering workshops and staff with light timetables. Apart from a small number of projects, usually for people in work, there was no concerted attempt to meet the training needs of an economy where, year by year,   manufacturing was declining, with rapid growth in service industries.

Apart from direct MSC funding to colleges for training, there was also the influence exerted through the Commission's control of 25 per cent of LEAs' further education budgets. This money had been transferred to the MSC because the government did not trust LEAs to develop appropriate education and training: it was given back only when LEAs/colleges produced plans which were considered satisfactory in terms of the government's training strategy. The planning exercises focused on the requirements of employers but resulted in no perceptible improvement in making training more relevant to the needs of a rapidly changing economy. The education and training needs of the unemployed were ignored or misunderstood.

Colleges were slow to respond to the curriculum needs of the unemployed as traditional manufacturing industries declined and the service sector expanded. Government and LEA policies continued as if unemployment was a short-term problem, which would quickly disappear with the next economic upturn. The priority of employers was to meet the short-term training needs of their workers : there was a general failure to recognise that there were major structural changes in the economy which only government could address. The more powerful training boards, such as engineering and construction, formed partnerships with colleges to address their own training needs but they could not be expected to assist people who wished to move from one vocational area to another. They also concentrated on teenage apprentice training and offered very limited opportunities for adults.

Instead of addressing the structural problems, which could have been done by legislation which created a new partnership between government and local authorities, with a framework which required the involvement of colleges in overall economic strategy, the government took steps to increase employer influence and to replace planning with the free operation of market forces. This strategy completely ignored the evidence of the 1960s/1980s, which demonstrates that failures in the training sphere make the development of further education appear an unqualified success story. Furthermore, although they clearly wish to exert influence on the training available for their own workers, there is no evidence that employers are anxious to determine the curriculum for the unemployed, or for students with special educational needs.

The 1988 Education Reform Act strengthened employer interest on governing bodies at the expense of LEAs and college staff. More significantly, it gave governing bodies effective control over college management and organisation. All LEAs were required to establish a scheme for the delegation of financial management, to be approved by the DES. The intention was to shift resources from curriculum areas of decline and reducing enrolment to support development in areas of demand (assumed to be a reflection of what employers and the economy needed). LEAs retained determination of strategy but colleges were given a high degree of independence in managing their resources, including staff. They were also encouraged to take income-generating initiatives, with *profits* retained for governors to spend.

A few LEAs accepted the spirit of the legislation. Unfortunately, but not unexpectedly, far too many continued to interfere in college management (which they were not entitled to do) but failed to develop a coherent strategic framework (which they were required to do). Resources were not systematically transferred from curriculum areas where they were being wasted to support expansion where there was demand. Most wasteful of all, in many areas small sixth forms were allowed to continue without any overall co-ordination of post-16 education and training.

An irritating (at least to LEAs) anomaly was that colleges had almost all employer powers, while the LEA remained the legal employer: for example, governing bodies were able to determine early retirements with enhanced pensions and redundancy payments but LEAs were required to finance them. Equally irritating (to colleges) was that some LEAs continued to strike agreements with trade unions without any reference to governors or college management.

Few would argue that the legal framework established by the 1988 Education Reform Act for governing relationships between LEAs and colleges was satisfactory. The action required was to establish governing body control of college management and development, and ensure that resources were made available on a fair basis to support expansion. There was no reason to remove LEA representatives from governing bodies, where they were already a minority. The other important issue was the process for determining strategy, especially to ensure that it related education and training to the economic, social and cultural needs of the area. Instead of requiring LEAs to take strategic planning more seriously, they were removed from the further education scene.

The main purpose of the reform of governing bodies after 1970 was to reduce political control over appointments. It was only partly successful because astute councillors could still control governing bodies: although in a minority, they were usually the only organised group. The balance of power shifted towards governors and college management after the 1988 Education Reform Act to a degree where councillors could not control appointments without the support of directors of education and principals. However, principally because they controlled budgets, LEAs were able to prevent colleges having the degree of independence the Act intended.

A more relevant solution would have been to give governors full corporate status to enable college management to manage without interference, apply a funding formula, but continue with elected local authority representatives (say 25 - 35 per cent) on corporations. This could have been accompanied by other arrangements for the election of a further 30 per cent of corporation members to guarantee a strong element of local accountability. Instead, all elected representatives were swept away and accountability was not even considered an issue.

The white paper *Education and Training* for the 21st Century and the Further and Higher Education Act, 1992

The publication of the white paper, especially because of its timing, was widely regarded as another attack by the government on local authorities. Incorporation of colleges would remove them from LEA control and there would no longer be LEA representation on governing bodies. From the outset, it was obvious that the main requirement - to raise the level of education and training and increase participation - would be undermined by a failure to create a unified system of education and training at 16 plus. School sixth forms would continue to exist alongside colleges; training would stay with the Department of Employment; non-vocational education would remain with local education authorities.

Equally alarming, funding would be controlled by a funding council (a quango), while strategy would be the responsibility of the new corporations (all quangos). There was no recognition in the white paper that the majority of students in colleges were adults, or that there were thousands of students who were neither full-time, nor day release, but unemployed and studying part-time (increasingly day rather than evening) without any financial support other than their social security benefit. It was also implicit that the curriculum divisions between the academic (GCE A level) and the vocational would continue.

The white paper ignored equal opportunities (Wymer, in Flint and Austin, 1994), which had been a priority of many local authorities in the 1980s: indeed, one of the government's grievances was that *loony left* councils had supported *gays* and *lesbians*. The emphasis was on the competence-based National Vocational Qualifications (NVQs), designed for people in work: there was no recognition of the Open College Network and the work of the regional federations (in association with polytechnics) in accrediting access to higher education courses for adults. It was difficult to escape the conclusion that the narrow vocationalism of the Department of Employment was about to be imposed on the whole of the further education sector. It was apparent that whoever drafted the white paper had very limited information about colleges, and was unaware of the contributions they made to the education and training of adults, including the unemployed. Neither was there evidence of any concern for the education and training needs of ethnic minority groups, many of whom had had a poor deal at school.

The most articulate opposition to the Bill which became the 1992 Further and Higher Education Act was from the adult and community education lobby. Although it did not prevent the marginalisation of non-vocational classes, the campaign established that adult education was much more than middle-class people playing badminton, or perfecting their flower arranging. Traditional programmes catering for leisure interests in middle-class communities were much better known than the more recent contributions to education and training for the unemployed. Also, there was a failure to recognise the relevance of education in the community as a first step in creating access to vocational studies. By transferring further education colleges, while leaving non-vocational adult education services with LEAs, the Act undermined collaboration and moves towards integration of vocational and non-vocational studies in some areas.

The most notable amendment to the Bill, from the House of Lords, required the Further Education Funding Council to ensure specific provision for students, including adults, with learning difficulties. This was accepted by Secretary of State Kenneth Clarke on the Second Reading of the Bill, perhaps because he was anxious to complete all stages before the general election. History may show that this was a bigger concession than he recognised. This is the only area of further education policy where the primary concern is the needs of the individual rather than the requirements of the economy/employers.

Although it was inadequately informed about colleges, the government was decisive about the intention of its further education policies.   The new corporations would be dominated by employment interests, with no real opportunity for wider community groups to contribute to policy evolution - either directly, or through elected local councillors.   The initial determination of membership was by the Secretary of State, with future determination a matter for the corporations themselves.   The question of accountability received scant attention: the government's position was that it should be to employers.   Although corporations were given responsibility for strategy, exposure to market forces was considered more likely than planning to result in the education and training necessary to re-generate the economy.

As already recorded in the introduction, the Labour Opposition was muddled about further education, not even sure whether it supported corporate status for colleges.   There was a loose alliance with local authorities, which did not want to lose control of colleges, but no strategy to increase participation, which all agreed was necessary to supply the training needs of industry in the 1990s, and to meet national education and training targets in terms of qualifications.   The Opposition was no more willing than the government to tackle the fundamental structural problems : the division between school sixth forms and colleges; the separate control of education and training; the separateness of vocational and non-vocational studies.

Further education colleges have an excellent record of offering a second chance to people who under-achieve at school and in meeting the training needs of employers.   If there was substantial evidence that colleges had failed to respond to demands articulated by employers it was not revealed.   The real situation, demonstrated in the operation of industrial training boards and the employer-dominated Manpower Services Commission, was that most employers had no interest beyond their short-term needs.   There is, however, plenty of evidence where employers have resisted curriculum designed to encourage a lifelong learning approach to training.   Yet this is precisely what is required to enable people to retrain and change their job several times in their working lives.

In addition to their work for employers, in some areas colleges have made outstanding contributions to the education and training of women previously denied access, ethnic minorities, people with learning difficulties. But during 1991 and 1992 college representatives proved completely incapable of making any significant contribution to the debate on the white paper and the Bill which resulted in the 1992 Further and Higher Education Act. It became alarmingly apparent that there was no effective national lobby for further education, contrasting with schools, adult education, the universities, public schools.

What could not be concealed was that the sector was divided. The Association of Colleges for Further and Higher Education represented the more traditional colleges; the Tertiary Colleges' Association spoke for tertiary colleges; the Sixth Form Colleges Association acted on behalf of sixth form colleges; the Association of Principals of Colleges acted for principals. The youngest organisation (some three years old), the Further Education Campaign Group, was the most vocal. Most of its members were also members of one or other of the established organisations and they worked hard to create a unified voice for the sector. Because this unity proved elusive in 1992, the government had no clear idea of the views of colleges and their governors on most of the major issues which had to be resolved.

Before the 1992 Act, LEAs were responsible for strategy, a duty exercised with varying degrees of commitment and competence, and sometimes not exercised at all. There was, generally, a failure to co-ordinate education and training at local level, reflecting the failure of government to co-ordinate the policies of the Department of Employment and the Department of Education and Science. The Act transferred responsibility for strategy to the new corporations, a meaningless gesture, as will be illustrated in the next chapter, when the Further Education Funding Council was given complete control of funding. Local authorities continued to control student support and training and enterprise councils retained local control over training for the employed and the unemployed. LEAs continued to control sixth forms, other than those in grant maintained and public schools.

Most colleges welcomed legal freedom from LEAs and some believed that the result would be independence. In many cases relationships with LEAs had deteriorated to a degree where almost any alternative seemed preferable. In their eagerness to acquire corporate status, colleges failed to recognise that the

Further Education Funding Council's control of funding would lead, inevitably, to effective control of strategy. As an agent of government policy, the FEFC would be obliged to give priority to provision leading to the narrow vocationalism of NVQs rather than the more student-oriented accreditation of, for example, the Open College Network. National control of funding would result in over-regulation and constant auditing. The government had re-invented the MSC, with the major difference that the new quango, as a near monopoly purchaser, would control the whole of further education provision.

Most serious of all in the longer term was the absence of any form of accountability for members of the new quangos. They would be responsible to nobody but themselves, with the power to sack chief executives, who were in turn given more powers than is good for them over staff. But few chief executives perceived that, caught uneasily between their corporations and the FEFC, they would be sitting ducks to become scapegoats when anything went wrong.

Corporations enjoined to stand on their own two feet soon discovered that they had to stand on their heads to comply with FEFC requirements. It also became apparent that they had no real powers if they attempted to move out of line with government policy - whatever the needs of their communities.

Issues resolved and unresolved

Although the timing of the 1992 Further and Higher Education Act may have been determined by the government's anti-local authority stance and preference for quangocracy over democracy, there was a growing consensus that action was necessary on post 16 education and training. The major factors to be addressed were:

(i)   the separate control of education and training at national and local level;

(ii)   the academic/vocational curriculum divide perpetuated by (i) above and impossible to resolve while it persisted;

(iii)   the separate control and funding of vocational and non-vocational studies;

(iv)   the division between school sixth-forms and colleges (except where tertiary colleges had been established) and between further education and sixth-form colleges;

(v)   the difficult, sometimes non-existent, relationship between LEAs and colleges, which thwarted sensible planning and efficient and effective use of resources.

These factors prevented the development of the education and training required for economic and social re-generation - in government policy terms they prevented the provision necessary for meeting national targets for education and training (NTET). Achieving the targets meant extending access to adults who had left school unqualified and received no education and training since: there was no chance of this while the divisions at 16 plus persisted.

The 1992 Further and Higher Education Act tackled only the college/LEA muddle, and, to some degree, the further education college/sixth form college divide - by making both part of the new further education sector. The chapters which follow will demonstrate that the transfer of colleges from LEA control was bungled, mainly because the necessary resolution of management responsibilities through granting colleges corporate status was accompanied by the unnecessary removal of all elements of democracy from the determination of corporation (governing body) membership. Furthermore, although LEAs had not been strikingly successful in the strategic planning sphere, they were in a stronger position to co-ordinate education and training than either college corporations or training and enterprise councils.

The separate control of education and training was not addressed by the Act. Three years later, the training responsibilities of the Department of Employment were transferred to the (re-named) Department for Education and Employment but the division at regional and local level remained, with colleges responsible for education and TECs responsible for training. The 1995 white paper *Competitiveness: Forging Ahead* gave TECs responsibility for *approving* colleges' strategic plans which, in legal terms, appeared to conflict with powers already given to corporations in their articles. As will be seen later, corporations are responsible for college strategic planning but it is a responsibility they are unable to exercise - because their funding is controlled by the Further Education Funding Council and local training strategy, such as it is, is controlled by the TECs.

The position on curriculum was made worse by the 1992 Act and the principles affirmed by its accompanying white paper. There was, of course, a consistency in the thrust towards vocationalism and the control of corporations, TECs, other related quangos, by business interests. The National Council for Vocational Qualifications, with its competency-based, employer-led, approach would, it was envisaged, take control of all qualifications, including higher education. It was clear at the time that narrow vocationalisation would neither provide suitable curriculum for the unqualified millions, nor result in the flexible workforce necessary for 21st century workers. The specific factor which prevented colleges responding to the needs of many in their communities was the 1992 Act's restriction of funding to curriculum leading to vocational qualifications.

The continuing unco-ordinated divisions between school sixth forms and colleges perpetuated duplication and waste of resources, with growing confusions for young people making choices at 16. Education and training is one of the best illustrations of how competition results in chaos rather than the free marketeers' claim of efficiency and choice. The most serious consequence of the 1992 Act's failure to create a unified, open access, system was that for millions of working-class people, the system the question of choice did not arise: there was no curriculum remotely relevant to their needs. Without an open access, unified structure, with the requirement of a coherent and customer responsive approach to curriculum, there is no chance of meeting even the modest targets of the government.

Of the five main issues noted earlier in this chapter, the 1992 Act tackled one and a half in the wrong manner. There are, obviously, pluses and minuses but, unless the unresolved questions are addressed urgently and emphatically by the government elected in 1997, the overall conclusion will be that the 1992 Act made matters worse than they would have been had there been no act at all. The Further Education Funding Council is a powerful juggernaut which is mechanically well-serviced and keeps going, but there will be serious consequences for colleges and their students if it continues to blunder along in the wrong policy direction.

Chapter Two

Corporations and their minders

Freedom and *independence* reverberated around Westminster in 1992. At a stroke, colleges would escape the shackles, bureaucracy, political interference of LEAs to be run by successful businessmen. Decisions, self-evidently correct ones, would be made quickly, waste cut out, and resources used to achieve national education and training targets. Efficiency would be guaranteed by competition in the market place, while the inefficient (presumably run by less successful businessmen) would go to the wall. The competition was quickly hotted up when schools were allowed to recruit adults, Secretary of State John Patten went on a sixth form creating bender, and the white paper, *Competitiveness: Forging Ahead* allowed, even encouraged, private education and training providers to apply directly to the Further Education Funding Council for funding.

The reality, foreseen by a minority but not widely recognised until after the second year of incorporation, was in stark contrast with the rhetoric. Far from being unrestricted free enterprise engines, the majority of corporations resembled leaded corks cast rudderless on a stormy sea. Enthusiasm drained from the most hardened businessmen when, having been subjected to innumerable circulars offering *advice* and (from corporations' angle pointless) audits, they received the regulations for the Private Finance Initiative (PFI) in 1995. The PFI regulations were so complex, if not self-contradictory, that (as correspondence at the time demonstrates) even government ministers could not understand them. Far from having the freedom necessary to meet the needs of their areas, corporations found themselves mangled cogs in a gigantic bureaucratic machine: the FEFC functioned as an LEA writ large and, as the largest customer for most colleges, controlled the education and training market.

Corporations and the Department for Education (DfE)

The DfE had the powers to approve the initial composition of corporations, which were then left to control their own membership. To the extent that anybody was responsible for corporations this was the Secretary of State but he/she was reluctant to exercise this responsibility and, in reality, had no effective means of doing so. No systematic arrangements were made for training corporation members and no guidance was given - for example, on the payment of corporation members. Although it was not clear whether or not payment was legal, the Colleges' Employers' Forum (CEF), advised by lawyers, took the view that it was and advised its members on rates. As a result a number of corporations agreed substantial payments for chairs and more modest rates for other members.

Over a year after the CEF's advice, the DfE and FEFC issued press statements on the same day taking the view, having been advised by lawyers, that payment was illegal. There was no challenge in the courts, no doubt for political reasons, and the DfE/FEFC interpretation, later confirmed in writing in a circular to colleges, came to be regarded as the position. This is, in principle, an unsatisfactory means of operation and the acceptance that the law is what the DfE, or FEFC (or both together) says it is one of the best illustrations of the dangers of departure from the democratic process. It is unlikely that the much maligned LEAs would have permitted payment of members but had they done so they would have been in a much better position to challenge the DfE and FEFC than individual corporations. Having issued the original advice on payment, the CEF, which was supposed to represent corporations, kept its head down.

Creating over 400 corporations and leaving them to their own devices meant that much was bound to go wrong and some of it came to light. The lack of accountability incited corporations to embark upon all sorts of enterprises, some of which had doubtful relevance to the education of students. The case which came to light was the functioning of the corporation at Derby Tertiary College, Wilmorton (Derbyshire), and it appears to have come to light because procedures were not followed rather than for the enterprises embarked upon. What Wilmorton demonstrated was that, without any process of accountability, a group of people thrown together, the majority from the business community, could prove less capable of the proper calling of meetings, taking minutes, observing constitutions than many a voluntary community organisation.

When the goings on at Wilmorton became public, the DfE had no idea what to do but the FEFC moved quickly to set up an enquiry headed by Michael Shattock. It is by no means self-evident that this action was either appropriate, or taken by the most appropriate body. The terms of reference for the enquiry ensured that when blame was apportioned it would be between college management (the principal) and corporation members, and that the DfE and FEFC would appear to be blameless.   Apart from its responsibilities for funding, the FEFC has a number of vague powers, not difficult to interpret as including the setting up of enquiries of the Wilmorton kind, and in any case it could be argued that there was some indication that its funds were not being properly used. But the legal powers and responsibilities of corporations pointed to the DfE, rather than the FEFC, as the proper initiator of such enquiries. The FEFC would, no doubt, argue both that there was a risk to funding and that its watchdog brief required it to act. This in no way alters the fact that initiatives of this kind lend credence to the view that the FEFC is responsible for corporations, and that corporations are accountable (in a general sense, not just on funding matters) to the FEFC. Although this notion has no clear basis in legislation, it is an illustration of how quangos acquire powers as a result of ministerial letters written in the context of legislation.   The intervention of *hidden hands* is a feature of quangocracy.

Predictably, given the terms of reference, the hatchet fell on the principal and corporation members when the Secretary of State accepted the recommendation of the FEFC based on the Shattock Report (FEFC, 1994). Equally predictably, there followed regulations and guidelines, including the proposal (not, ultimately, implemented) that corporation clerks should become secret agents for, in effect, the FEFC.   There was a great deal of pious talk about accountability, including some from the government which had removed it with the 1992 Act. The FEFC adopted a code of conduct to regulate the operation of its own council members and recommended corporations to do the same - a sort of voluntary accountability. Although there is no reason to question that the vast majority of corporation members are anxious to behave well, one of the messages of Wilmorton is that, in the absence of democratic accountability, there is no community leverage to inhibit bad education and training decisions - providing they are taken in accord with procedures.

The most disturbing outcome of Wilmorton is that, although the enquiry found nothing illegal; the principal and corporation members were dismissed without reasonable opportunities to present their sides of the story. The situation at the college was undoubtedly chaotic, and the facts indicate that the institution was not run in the best interests of staff or students. Corporation members lacked training and there was no effective process of principal accountability. But who was responsible for training members? It cannot be argued that the principal was responsible for training his bosses, but the absence of member training, it could be argued, was the reason for the absence of a process for principal accountability. The responsibility for the Wilmorton debacle must be placed firmly on the legislation which created the quangos and the Department responsible for implementing it.

By stepping in swiftly with its enquiry the FEFC was able to impose terms of reference which determined that it would not be blamed for the mess. If the Council is responsible for sorting out problems of the Wilmorton kind, it must also share responsibility for not preventing them - in this case for not providing training and assistance with running corporations. The DfE, latterly the DfEE, accountable to the electorate for its action (or inaction), no doubt perceives some advantage in shuffling off responsibilities to a quango. Because the FEFC determined the terms of reference of the inquiry, the Council escaped criticism and the axe fell, predictably, on the principal and corporation members. The exercise demonstrated that, to the extent that corporation members are accountable to anybody but themselves, they are answerable to another quango, the FEFC, not the community they serve.

The other major government responsibility, additional to creating the legal framework for colleges, is the requirement for majority control of corporations by employer representatives. The principled objection is not to the employer members as such but to the fact that, providing they keep within the bounds of the law and common sense, they are accountable to nobody but themselves. For all the objections to LEA governors, and it has to be accepted that they did not always function in the best interests of colleges, they could, ultimately, be thrown out by the electorate. Since 1993 employer members and, indeed, all members, can be dismissed only by a majority vote of the corporation - in effect, by the employers themselves.

Nobody would challenge a legitimate employer interest and it is vitally important that their training requirements are consistently addressed. Yet where is the evidence that employer requests for training were in any respect neglected before the 1988 Education Reform Act? Training has always been good business for colleges and LEAs and the record shows that, historically, college resources have been made available to employers on a large scale, especially in areas such as construction and engineering. In some colleges there is a history of excluding full-time students and the unemployed from classes offered for employers, even where fees were heavily subsidised by the LEA.

Beyond the direct employer interest - for example, on basic education, special educational needs, GCE A level, non-vocational education - on what grounds is it assumed that employers views are any more, or less, valuable than anybody else's? Employers do not have, and would not claim to have, any special expertise in these areas, and where they have an involvement or commitment it is normally expressed in the form of support for professionals with experience and knowledge. The notion that employers need a majority on corporations to implement their policies on special educational needs or non-vocational education is bizarre. Although businesses have training policies for their managers and workers, which include policies not to train, they are unlikely to have policies on special educational needs and non-vocational education.

The inescapable conclusion is that the idea that colleges are better governed with an employer majority is pure ideology without any support from history or practice. There is a world of difference between recognising that colleges need to be more businesslike and running them like a steel stockholders or a bank. The positive and helpful contributions on corporations come from the employer members who are able to make their experience and expertise count precisely because they understand that a college is not a steel stockholders or a bank. The greatest benefits to colleges result when employers are willing to become involved in partnerships with colleges, with each side recognising its own limitations and its partner's strength.

The damage resulting from control by one interest, whether employer or other, is illustrated by the history of training since the 1960s. The 1964 Industrial Training Act placed training firmly in the hands of employers, operating through industrial training boards. They remained the dominant party through the period of the Manpower Services Commission and the Department of Employment agencies (TSA, TEED) which succeeded it. The effect was to allow the employer influence to determine the shape of training for the unemployed as well as the employed. Employers, as other interested parties, like their views on training for the unemployed to be known but there was never any evidence of their wish to control it. Almost all the training schemes for the unemployed in the 1980s and 1990s failed, mainly because school-leavers and adults were offered a watered down form of vocational training designed for people in work, mainly in traditional industries. It is now recognised that what was required was basic skills training to enable people to reach the level necessary to undertake vocational training, and new provision for emerging job areas, especially in the service sector.

Only a government out of touch with reality and blinded by ideology could reach the conclusion that the country's record on training pointed to handing control of further education to employers. A three-way partnership (employers, community, college), as existed before the 1988 Education Reform Act, would have been much more appropriate for addressing the education and training needs of the unqualified and unemployed, without any risk that employers' training needs would be neglected. The case for local councillor members of corporations is that they are accountable to an electorate, although it is recognised that there can be conflict of interest difficulties. The most appropriate solution is direct elections for one third of corporations members, a process which would do a great deal to raise the profile of colleges in their communities, as well as to ensure accountability.

The Thatcher governments considered quangos controlled by businessmen (the Tory alternative to local authorities run by the loony left) the answer to all problems, whether in health, social services, transport, education. Whatever the issue, the views of businessmen (and a few businesswomen) were given the greatest weight. It is not easy to find examples where this led to improvement of services, but there are plenty of examples where the quality of service declined. The blind faith in the business experience, very different from the appointment of businessmen on merit, resulted in the kind of scepticism expressed by Dan Atkinson in *The Guardian* at the beginning of 1996:

> Name a dud or dubious cause, and spokesmen for "business opinion" will, like as not, have been pushing it hard. Motorway building (nice soft contracts), youth training schemes (nice subsidised workforce), the Common Market (nice large consumer base), the ERM (nice fashionable idea, perfect for "business opinion) and the current bill to move British clocks on to Reich Standard Time (certain to win "business" backing, combining, as it does, several dud ideas in one).

> The suits' cause-of-causes is the single currency, which they claim is vital to the ability of British industry to compete in Europe. Unfortunately, British industry couldn't compete in Europe even if all its rivals were knocked out by a Sarin gas attack, hence our visible

trade balance with the Union, which has deteriorated inexorably from a surplus of under £1 billion in 1980 to a deficit of £4 billion now.

Despite this dismal performance, British business is determined to bring its non-talents to the prison service, the railways, the Post Office and the national health service. Anti-Business Year will change all that. Let's all raise our glasses to the New year toast: *The Anti-Enterprise Culture!*

It was Margaret Thatcher who established the cult of the tycoonery with her oft quoted "Everyone else brings me problems. David (Young) brings me solutions". Lord Young eventually became a problem and was dropped from the government but the cult prospered, as did some of the individuals appointed to well-paid quango posts. Apart from the fact that there is no democratic accountability, business control does not appear to improve service. Andrew Rawnsley's comments (*Observer* 16 June 1996) are probably a fair summary:

> For 17 years the powers of local authorities have been sucked away and transferred to unelected representatives of the tycoonery - all in the name of bringing entrepreneurial flair to the running of public bodies. Businessmen have been given urban development agencies and National Health Service trusts to play with. Schools, further education colleges and police authorities, too. It has to be said that they have not been strikingly better managed as a result. Investigations by the National Audit Office, and others who invigilate the quangocracy, have uncovered unprecedented levels of inefficiency, malpractice and plain corruption.

Corporations and the Further Education Funding Council   (FEFC)

The 1992 Act gave corporations powers as absolute as companies, subject only to the over-riding powers of the Secretary of State in the event of improper behaviour. Technically corporations are exempt trusts, which means that they do not have to make returns to the Charities' Commissioner: annual accounts are returned to the FEFC. The Further Education Funding Council was established to distribute the government's funding for vocational education, which was transferred from local education authorities in 1993. It was also given the responsibility to assess the adequacy of education provision for 16-18 year-olds and make recommendations to the Secretary of State - for example, on the opening, or closure, of sixth forms.

The main responsibilities of corporations, which cannot be delegated to committees or principals, are described in the *Articles of Government* (HMSO, 1992), as:

(i)   the determination of the educational character and mission of the institution;

(ii)   the approval of the annual estimates of income and expenditure;

(iii)   ensuring the solvency of the institution and the corporation and the safeguarding of their assets;

(iv)   the appointment or dismissal of the principal; and

(v)   the modifying or revoking of the Articles.

The level of independence exercised by college governing bodies following the 1988 Education Reform Act varied enormously. Some were run by LEAs as if they were schools; others appointed their own clerks and were allowed to operate with a high degree of independence from the LEA. The director of education continued to have the right to attend meetings and present reports. Some colleges without experience of running their own governing bodies encountered considerable difficulties following incorporation: the Wilmorton case demonstrates that even the basic requirement of issuing agenda on time and producing minutes proved too much.

The most serious problems arose where corporation members believed their independence was absolute, a not unreasonable conclusion given the 1992 government statements about the free market economy and escape from LEA shackles. In reality, whether corporations were run well, or badly, depended a great deal on principals and chairs, particularly on whether they pulled together or in different directions. In practice almost everything could be delegated to principals, or principals in consultations with chairs. Given the rapid changes which followed incorporation, and the demands of the FEFC, it was almost impossible to place all major issues before corporations until after deadlines had passed. This applied to the spending of hundred of thousands of pounds on buildings, student returns, bids for growth. The reason the DfE and the FEFC were unconcerned about this situation was that the decisions, which legally belonged to corporations, were, in effect, made by the FEFC.

The FEFC was established to take responsibility for funding, not strategy, which was clearly the responsibility of corporations under the 1992 Further and Higher Education Act.   The expression of corporation policies, and the proposals for implementing them, are described in the strategic plan.   In theory the plan should give priority to addressing the education and training needs of the area: in practice, it cannot avoid giving priority to what the Further Education Funding Council will fund.   This is work described in Schedule II of the Further and Higher Education Act as:

(a)   a course which prepares students to obtain a vocational qualification which is, or falls within a class, for the time being approved for the purposes of this sub-paragraph by the Secretary of State,

(b)   a course which prepares students to qualify for:-

(i)   the General Certificate of Secondary Education, or
(ii)   the General Certificate of Education at Advanced Level or Advanced Supplementary Level (including Special Papers),

(c)   a course for the time being approved for the purposes of this sub-paragraph by the Secretary of State which prepares students for entry to a course of higher education,

(d)   a course which prepares students for entry to another course falling within paragraphs (a) to (c) above,

(e)   a course for basic literacy in English,

(f)   a course to improve the knowledge of English of those for whom English is not the language spoken at home,

(g)   a course to teach the basic principles of mathematics,

(h)   in relation to Wales, a course for proficiency or literacy in Welsh,

(j)   a course to teach independent living and communication skills to persons having learning difficulties which prepares them for entry to another course falling within paragraphs (d) to (h) above.

The list of qualifications eligible for FEFC funding is published by the Secretary of State, and updated from time to time. It tends to give the highest weighting to traditional vocational qualifications. As stated in an earlier chapter, qualifications evolved to recognise the individual's attainment and progress, such as those of the Open College Network, are generally given a lower weighting, at least in the first instance. College certificates were recognised for FEFC funding purposes 1993/96, providing they marked progress towards a qualification on the DfEE list. After 1996 the only student programmes not requiring a DfEE listed qualification were at basic skills level.

The new funding methodology introduced by the FEFC in 1994 was a major advance on the system used by the Department of Education and Science to fund local education authorities - especially the allowances for students who were unemployed and for people with learning difficulties. Unfortunately, it was applied, blindly, to all colleges, with no opportunity for corporation discretion. What could have been a progressive step - for example, if the methodology had been applied with 80 per cent direct funding of students and 20 per cent for corporation discretion - became a straight jacket. Because the setting of targets and payments were based on traditional further education criteria, colleges which did not conform to the norm were at a disadvantage. For example, the minority of colleges which enrolled more students in the summer than in the autumn were penalised because payment profiles were based on the assumption that more students enrolled in the autumn.

The necessity to apply criteria mechanistically, and an inability to take account of problems where colleges did not conform to the national norm, were directly related to the fact that powers were concentrated at the centre. Because regional committees and regional officers were given no powers their function was merely to implement decisions made by the national council and national officers. Instead of assessing the needs of their localities and then attempting to meet them, colleges had no option but to offer only what the FEFC would fund. The Council also determined the framework for strategic plans and then used them to control colleges and their provision. The most serious consequence was to make colleges less responsive to education and training needs in their localities.

For most colleges, the FEFC became the biggest contractor. Local authorities, which continued to fund non-vocational provision (in many cases in colleges), were under financial pressure and in most areas funding was reduced year by year. The division between vocational and non-vocational curriculum had never had much meaning for students but from the 1980s many adult education services had made significant contributions to, for example, return to study courses for the unemployed and for women returners. Although after 1993 some of this work was accredited for FEFC funding, the distinction between vocational and non-vocational made it extremely difficult for corporations to develop coherent strategies. Where LEAs continued to offer vocational courses as part of their adult education services this was funded by the FEFC through an incorporated college.

The government's intention in 1992 was to make colleges compete in the market place like any other business. It was assumed that freedom from local authority control would enable them to act where previously they had been restricted. In fact, the FEFC introduced more regulations than ever experienced before and intervened in the market. Lack of knowledge and understanding of further education, most notable in the community education sphere, did not hinder its intervention, which in a number of instances had the effect of undermining corporation strategy.

One of the best examples of the FEFC's lack of understanding was on European funding. European Social Fund (ESF) Objective III, for example, was based on the principle of *additionality*. This meant that bodies acquiring it, including colleges, were expected to use the income for enhancement and extension of provision - for the long-term unemployed, people with learning difficulties etc - not as a substitute for mainstream funding. Yet for every ESF funded student the FEFC deducted European grant from mainstream funding, contrary to European Commission intentions. Because most European funding is allocated to areas of high unemployment, a number of which have substantial numbers of ethnic minorities, the way in which the clawback operated did not assist the *additionality* contribution to equal opportunities.

In areas of high unemployment European sources offered the best opportunity for colleges to acquire funding not *controlled* by the FEFC and the government's vocationalism. The criteria for Objective II and Objective III Social Funds place emphasis on involvement of communities and lifelong education; a direct contrast with the narrow vocationalism of Schedule II of the 1992 Further and Higher Education Act. In 1996, when it was decided that

Objective III would be regionalised in 1997, the FEFC, which had administered Objective III for the further education sector when it was operated nationally, decided to opt out.

The European emphasis on the regions is contrary to the FEFC's commitment to a highly regulated national system. The Council's general half-heartedness about European funding reflected the government's ambivalence about Europe.

In general, the powers of corporations were heavily circumscribed with regulations, with the FEFC using its control of the government's further education funding to determine strategy. Where it could not apply regulations, it attempted to operate through audit. It regarded its word as law and in the event of disagreement there was no means of appeal - except to the courts. Because colleges do not have a national collective voice, any dispute with the FEFC amounts to a small quango with no resources battling with a large quango with, for the purpose of such a battle, unlimited resources.

It is easy to argue that the LEAs' loss of further education was no more than they deserved. Their failure to develop sensible strategies, or recognise the necessity for colleges to be managed on site rather than from the education office, caused muddle and conflict which resulted in waste of precious resources. It was not surprising that many governors, and most principals, were delighted to escape. But councillors *do* represent communities and every four years the electorate *do* have the opportunity to throw them out. If they persistently ignore needs and aspirations they pay the price. As governors they were accountable to the electorate, and this accountability extended to their involvement with further education colleges. Although this aspect of the democratic process may not have seemed to amount to very much in some areas, it existed as an ultimate safeguard.

The FEFC has a range of advisory committees and a process of consultation which elicits common denominators but is incapable of taking into account the realities and needs of individual colleges. Consultations are by carefully planned survey and it would be surprising if there has ever been an exercise where the FEFC did not know the outcome in advance. The whole process is based on the assumption that the sector will function satisfactorily if all colleges operate in accord with a number of mechanistic parameters. In terms of complying with FEFC regulations the historical strengths of colleges - their responsiveness to community need and, hence, their diversity - have become weaknesses.

Their *Articles* give corporations what appear to be far-reaching powers. In reality, these amount to very little when funding depends on strict compliance with FEFC edicts. The devil, as usual, in the details, exemplified in paragraphs such as:

> The Corporation shall - comply with any directions given by the appropriate Further Education Funding Council as to the information contained in it (the audit), the manner in which the information is to be presented, the methods and principles according to which it is prepared and the time and manner of publication (HMSO, 1992).

Although, in law, this does not give the FEFC powers to do what it thinks fit, in practice it is known that corporations are unlikely to take court action. In 1996, for example, the FEFC unilaterally ignored the funding agreement signed by colleges and refused to pay for growth above 30 per cent (the *Demand-Led Element*). The Circular stating a number of new requirements, introduced retrospectively, was accepted by most colleges as a statement of the legal position, rather than the breach of contract it obviously was.

Where there is disagreement, there is no machinery for resolving disputes. If the FEFC does not agree, it merely withholds funding. *Democratic* decisions, whether of corporations or communities, are completely ignored. Despite the legal position as stated in the *Articles*, many corporation members quickly reach the conclusion that they are, in reality, accountable to the Further Education Funding Council and must observe all its regulations.

Corporations and chief executives (principals)

Between 1992 and 1996 over 100 chief executives departed, a higher fatality rate than managers of football clubs and with, comparatively, insignificant compensation. Any change as major as incorporation is likely to result in new top managers and the retirement of college chief executives by mutual agreement might have been expected to result in a change of 50-60. But natural change cannot explain the departure of over 100. There is no intention here to defend incompetent managers, or imply that chief executives should have special treatment. But to the extent that there are problems in the legal framework that are likely to continue to cause difficulty there are implications for the service that need to be addressed.

The *Articles of Government* give chief executives far-reaching responsibilities and, it must be assumed, the powers to exercise them:

a)   for making proposals to the corporation about the educational character and mission of the institution, and for implementing the decisions of the corporation;

b)   for the organisation, direction and management of the institution and leadership of the staff;

c)   for the appointment, assignment, grading, appraisal, suspension, dismissal, and determination, *within the framework set by the corporation*, of the pay and conditions of service, of staff other than the holders of senior posts;

d)   for the determination, after consultation with the Academic Board, of the institution's academic activities, and for the determination of its other activities;

e)   for preparing annual estimates of income and expenditure, for consideration and approval by the corporation, and for the management of budget and resources, within the estimates approved by the corporation, and

f)   for the maintenance of student discipline and, within the rules and procedures provided for within these Articles, for the suspension or expulsion of students on disciplinary grounds and for implementing decisions to expel students for academic reasons.

One difficulty is that the responsibilities are explicit, the powers implicit. They are, however, given by the Secretary of State, not the corporation, and it follows that the corporation cannot remove them. Separate and additional to those stated in the *Articles* are the powers delegated to chief executives by corporations which can, of course, be re-claimed.

No college can function effectively unless the chief executive and corporation reach a common understanding of the position and record it in, and around, the contract of service. On a day-to-day basis very few decisions will require a decision of the corporation, or even the involvement of the chair. Yet it is a foolish chief executive who does not consult the chair regularly, or who does not provide corporations with the information on which important decisions are based. Whatever the division of powers, a corporation cannot meet its obligations without a competent chief executive, and a chief executive cannot be successful without corporation support.

Because a chief executive cannot have policies different from the policies of the corporation, it is essential for all members to feel a sense of ownership of decisions, and to be fully aware of the implications of implementation. During the 1993 to 1996 period it was not unusual for chief executives to find themselves in an uneasy sandwich between trade unions and corporation members; sometimes with fatal consequences. A *Times Educational Supplement* report (*Row follows "colonels' revolt"*) is an example:

> Lecturers at Southampton City College have passed a vote of no confidence in the chairs of the college corporation and employment policy committee following the suspension of the principal.

> The college's branch of the lecturers' union NATFHE claims staff have been left in the dark over the decision by governors, which came after a "colonels' revolt" of senior staff opposed to plans for reform, including management redundancies.

> A management team now running the college has refused to speak about an inquiry launched following the principal's suspension.

> The NATFHE branch secretary, claimed the union had been warned off commenting publicly on the inquiry. He said: "These managers are saying we are all going to pull together for the college but when we ask for even minimal assurances about the future we are denied them. We will not be gagged just because they are not prepared to tell us the issues".

> The union fears that if a new principal is sought, the costs involved in a change could further jeopardise the finances of the college, which is already struggling with £1.2million debts.

The principal was appointed three years ago after head-hunters were brought in at the college. His suspension has sparked alarm in the Association of Principals of Colleges, which claims chief executives can be too easily driven out by under-trained but powerful governors.

A common experience is for corporation agreement to reduce staffing costs, followed by strong union reaction and representations to members when redundancies are announced by the chief executive. Threats of industrial action and votes of no confidence in college management and the corporation then cause a corporation change of mind to meet union demands. In most cases of difficulty it can be shown that the chief executive, in announcing redundancies, is in accord with a democratic decision. Where a change of mind occurs, leaving the chief executive on a limb, it is frequently the case that the issues were not properly debated when the original decision was taken. Whether the fault is with the chief executive, or the chair, the inescapable fact, when difficulties of this kind arise, is that the two leaders have not established an effective working relationship.

Probably more common is where chief executives are caught between the FEFC and corporations, usually on matters related to finance and target achievement. The apparent smooth and systematic approach to budget allocation is a veneer which conceals the fact that a rigid mechanistic blunderbuss is incapable of taking into account crucial factors affecting individual colleges. There are, of course, factors common to almost all colleges but a system which assumes all colleges have everything in common is a monumental absurdity.   When difficulties arise, corporation decisions are ignored by the FEFC and, as already stated, there is no means of resolving disputes, other than in court. When there is a dispute between a corporation and the FEFC the most likely scapegoat is the chief executive.

The last bureaucratic straw is the knowledge that a college cannot obtain its FEFC budget allocations unless a funding agreement is signed. This is not, in fact, an *agreement* but a document written by the FEFC with no college input. Even when agreements are signed they are changed unilaterally, without consultation, as for example on demand-led element payments 1995/96 already described. The general position is one of a big quango grinding little quangos into submission: decisions of corporations, however democratically taken, count for nothing.

The whole process is the implementation of government policy through a quango. The FEFC operates Stalinistically, and is structurally incapable of resolving issues raised by corporations, other than in a mechanistic sense through a formula. The policy requirement to fund only courses leading to vocational qualifications ignores the education and training needs of millions of people, especially adults, for whom the only means of access is through community education. The absence of democratic control or accountability at any level prevents articulation of the curriculum requirements of more than half the adult population. This is the issue addressed in the chapters which follow.

Chapter Three

Community colleges and educating the community

The evolution of community colleges

The United Kingdom education system is dominated, and still controlled, by people committed to academic, elitist traditions. In further education recent years have seen the vocationalists' influence grow, partly as the result of government policy of increasing employer representation on quangos, including corporations. Oxford, Cambridge, public schools, grammar schools continue largely uninfluenced by twentieth century developments in education. The majority of managers at senior levels in the civil service, local government, universities, schools - and even colleges of further education - were educated at grammar or public schools and one of the old universities (as opposed to the promoted polytechnics).   They belong to an elite who accept that some expansion of further and higher education is necessary but they are not committed to education and training for all. Their vision is of a meritocracy, a rationing of expansion, with success dependent on the achievement of qualifications where standards are considered to depend on percentage pass and failure rates, rather than the attainment of individuals.

Vocational traditions in English education developed separately from academic traditions and largely outside the state system, for example in trade schools in the nineteenth century. From the 1850s, the Department of Science and Arts, as a matter of policy and principle, gave grants to private organisations to develop adult education and training:

> The work thus done is mainly done by the public itself on a self supportary basis as far as possible, whilst the state avoids the error of the continental system, of taking the principal part.[1]

When county colleges, envisaged by the 1944 Education Act as providing part-time further education for all 16-18 year olds not in full time study, failed to get off the ground, further education became increasingly influenced by employers. Following the 1964 Industrial Training Act, industrial training boards dominated until they were superseded by the Manpower Services

Commission, the Training Services Agency and its successors, and now the training and enterprise councils.   The 19th century principle of funding training separately from education has continued throughout the whole period.

The resistance to change of both academic and vocational traditions is demonstrated by the fact that there are still two, separate, examination systems. Although the Dearing Report, *Review of Qualifications for 16-19 Year Olds* (SCAA, 1996), attempts to establish a framework to embrace both, too much is conceded to the academics.   Abolishing A levels, the only means towards a unified, comprehensive, examination system is not on the Dearing agenda because it is considered politically unacceptable.   This is a reflection of the extent to which elitism continues to control the educational and political establishment.

Although all generalisations about the further education system must be treated with caution, colleges may be divided, broadly, into two categories: technical colleges with a strong vocational bias and further education (including tertiary) colleges more closely associated with school traditions.   A third group, sixth form colleges, now in the further education sector are similar to those tertiary colleges enrolling mainly full time students, and there are still specialist colleges (e.g. agriculture) which have not merged with further education colleges.   Until the 1980s, community colleges - for example in Cambridgeshire and Leicestershire - were based on schools linked to LEA adult education services, and were regarded as extensions of schools, not as part of the further education system.

Bilston Community College (1984) has always claimed to be the first open access community college under further education regulations.   It has never been demonstrated that this claim is inaccurate, although FEFC inspectors were too cautious to record it in their report, substituting the safer *one of the first.*   Since 1990 a growing number of colleges have introduced "community" into their titles, usually a signal that they intend to enrol large numbers of individuals from the community, as distinct from part-time students sent by employers, or full-timers transferring from schools at 16.   The Further Education Funding Council uses the term *independent* to describe these students.

The best known community colleges are in the USA, established by President Truman after the second world war to help ordinary people over 18 realise the American dream.   They offer courses on an open access basis to millions of adults, who are able to study on a full-time or part-time basis and, over two years, accumulate credits towards a diploma: this enables them to transfer to a university and acquire a degree over a further two years. The curriculum is broadly-based, with little vocationalism of the narrow kind found in English colleges. There are, however, close working relationships with the business community, which does not expect vocationalism to dominate the curriculum in colleges. An interesting recent development in the USA is the number of vocational colleges, usually established to serve a particular industry (e.g. motor, aircraft), which are broadening their curriculum base and adopting community-college-type open access policies.

There is an undoubted USA community college influence on those English colleges which have become open access and expanded provision for adults enrolling as individuals during the past decade. Unemployment has persisted at, on average, three times the level of the 1960s and a growing number of the unemployed recognise that they are unlikely to find jobs without recognised qualifications. The numbers enrolling on their own initiative at a time when day release, and in some areas school-leaver numbers, have declined has encouraged colleges to focus more on the education and training needs of people in their communities. The fact that much of this new demand is from adults means that those colleges which have historically concentrated on 16-18s are having to re-examine their strategies.

The training schemes initiated directly by the Department of Employment in the 1970s and, later, through its agencies such as the Manpower Services Commission, were mostly short term - designed more to keep people off the unemployment register than to provide genuine education and training leading to recognised qualifications. The involvement of colleges varied from area to area but regulations did not permit study for educational qualifications such as GCE A level. In areas of high unemployment local authorities attempted, usually through colleges, to make relevant provision for the jobless - in some cases with European Social Fund support. As unemployment persisted at a disturbingly high level, with no real prospect of improvement - especially where heavy manufacturing industry was disappearing never to return - it became apparent that traditional further education, academic and vocational, was not appropriate for many citizens. This applied especially to those who had left school at the earliest opportunity and had participated in no education or training since - well over fifty per cent of the adult population.

The training schemes of the 1970s and 1980s were inadequate because there was a failure to recognise major structural changes in the economy. The schemes were short-term because it was assumed that, as in the 1950s and 1960s, an economic upturn was just round the corner and full employment would return. The insistence on giving priority to employer-based training ignored the needs of the unemployed and the fact that the rapidly changing economy required an emphasis on re-training for workers to transfer, for example, from manufacturing to the expanding service sector. For obvious reasons, it has always been an absurdity to thrust upon employers responsibility for education and training for the unemployed or for people moving from one industry to another.

Despite comprehensive secondary education and the expansion of colleges, large numbers of working class people continued to acquire more education in their communities than in the state system. By 1990 this applied particularly to significant numbers of Asian and Afro-Caribbean teenagers, many of whom had found little of relevance in their school experience. Youth clubs, community centres, places of worship, trade unions, women's institutes are merely some examples of the agencies of community education. Some voluntary organisations received grants from LEAs, and for a period in the 1970s and 1980s from the Department of Employment youth and adult training scheme community projects. Links with further education colleges occurred in some cases but the short-termness of the funding meant that there were very few opportunities for students/trainees to progress to higher levels of study. The training allowances were available for only vocational study, not access to further or higher education.

By the time the 1992 Act reached the statute book it was clear that the vocational and academic traditions could not provide a relevant education and training for all, or even sufficient numbers to achieve national education and training targets. Technical and further education colleges, historically dominated by these traditions, needed to become community colleges and offer education for the community, in the community, to create access for people who left school completely alienated by the system. The priority in 1992 was not to extend vocationalism but to recognise and develop a community education curriculum, with the emphasis on basic skills for the millions whose needs were largely ignored by the traditional curriculum leading to recognised vocational qualifications.

The need for community education

The number of school leavers staying on in education increased steadily in the 1980s and early 1990s, to the point where it was claimed that over 80 per cent of 16-17 year olds were in either education, training or work. This represented a catching up on competitor nations, although the UK remained well behind for post 17s and adults. Whereas in Germany, for example, over two thirds of the workforce had a recognised qualification, this applied to only one third of the United Kingdom workforce.

Apart from the participation rate, there are serious questions about the quality and relevance of what is offered to 16-17 year olds. Of those who stay on full-time, there is significant drop out and a 25 per cent failure rate in GCE A levels. Some young people join youth training schemes not because they are interested but because they receive training allowances, not available if they continue in full-time education. As the Dearing Report, *Review of Qualifications for 16-19 Year Olds*, confirms, many leave without a recognised qualification or a job: the figures indicating greater participation conceal the fact that many derive no long-term benefit from their training. The greatest concern is for those who go missing after they leave school, poor because if they do not join a training scheme they receive no social security benefits.

Reports produced by the National Youth Agency (1995), the Home Office (1995), the TEC National Council (1996), the Adult Literacy and Basic Skills Unit (ALBSU) (1995), Bilston Community College (1996) provide evidence from which it can be concluded that there are around 10 million people over 14 who require education and training with at least some basic skills support. A report by the TEC National Council, *Disaffection and non-participation in education, training and employment by individuals aged 18 - 20* (1996), revealed that in 1995 there were 227,600 18-20 year olds in neither education, training nor work. The ALBSU report points to 6 million adults requiring basic skills, and a large proportion of the registered disabled (again over 6 million) are in need of education and training. Even accepting that there is some overlap in these figures, the number in need of further education and training with basic skills support cannot be far short of 10 million.

This is not just a matter of skills shortages in the economy, the almost sole pre-occupation of the government when it introduced the 1992 Further and Higher Education Act, serious as this is. Although the consequences of so many people being, in effect, excluded from society do not appear to be of major concern to the UK government, the European Commission is seriously concerned, as is illustrated by the recent white paper *Teaching and Learning:Towards the Learning Society*

> Long term unemployment continues to increase and the spread of social exclusion, particularly among young people, has become a major problem in our societies. The white paper takes the view that in modern Europe the three essential requirements of social integration, the enhancement of employability and personal fulfilment are not incompatible.

Neither is the complacency of the UK government shared by public servants whose work brings them into contact with the underclass of the excluded. A chief constable, for example, was reported (*The Guardian*, 4 May 1996) as follows:

> An electronic underclass, denied access to the information super highway society, is being created and could cause major problems of crime and disorder, a senior police officer has warned.

> While the wealthy will be able to shop, bank, enjoy live entertainment and even vote electronically from home, an alienated group could haunt the wasteland of the future, suggests David Blakey, chief constable of West Mercia and secretary of the Association of Chief Police Officers' crime committee.

> Writing in the latest ACPO journal, Policing Today, Mr Blakey says that in the future the educated will have "the money, the means and skills to access any information in the world". But below that level an electronic underclass could be created.

> This underclass will be alienated, denied access to the new society because of lack of education and wealth", he says. "They will haunt the now empty shopping and entertainment areas, causing major problems for the police and for the rest of society. That process is already taking place, he argues".

College expansion of over 16 per cent in the first three years of incorporation (1993/96) has not, except in isolated cases, reached out to people excluded in the sense that these reports describe. The main reason is the government's policy emphasis on vocationalism, largely irrelevant to the majority of excluded people, in further education and on academic A levels in school sixth forms.

The case for community education curriculum, with education and training in the community to create access for the unqualified, the unemployed, people with learning difficulties, was not recognised during the debates leading up to the 1992 Further and Higher Education Act and it continues to be rejected or ignored.

The community education alternative

It is the commitment of the establishment to meritocracy, a rationing by the imposition of academic and vocational traditions, which excludes large numbers of young people and adults from education and training. A meritocracy prevents the development of potential by arranging that people succeed only if they conform and adapt to the system. It treats people with low attainment as inferior, rather than as individuals with talents to be developed. The conventional wisdom that qualifications must be acquired at a certain age - GCSEs at 16, GCE A levels at 18 - takes no account of the support needed by many who have been denied opportunities at school. Expansion on the principle of meritocracy means that benefits are mainly to the middle classes, with exclusion of the majority of the working classes from anything other than short-term training schemes. The growth in the number of working class people in higher education, for example, can easily conceal the fact that their percentage of the higher education population has not changed dramatically.

Community education curriculum, and the provision of education and training in the community, is the only means of creating access for excluded teenagers and most of the adults who left school unqualified. Community education traditions originated as deep in history as the vocational and academic traditions but they have been, and are, available largely outside the statutory education system. Any contact has been, and is, on the margins - for example, in association with LEA adult education services, or university extra mural departments. For a brief period in the 1980s the Manpower Services Commission supported youth and adult training projects in the community, with sufficient funding for training in colleges, but this support disappeared when the Job Training Scheme was introduced in 1987.

Space does not permit tracing the history of community education from the wandering minstrels of the middle ages; making the case that Shakespeare's pre-eminence results from the fact that he drew heavily on it; describing its social importance from the period of the levellers in the seventeenth century to the chartists of the nineteenth. The importance of community education associated with community history is recognised in the work of Christopher Hill, E P Thompson and Raymond Williams. Its flavour in the nineteenth century is captured most strikingly by R H Tawney, in *The Radical Tradition* (Pelican, 1964), when he describes the discussion groups arranged by trade unions, co-operatives, friendly societies, chapels. Tawney describes the leaders of these groups as

> humble men and women whose names are remembered lovingly in their own little towns and villages

The challenge facing further education as the millennium approaches is that there are still hundreds of thousands, probably millions, of working-class people in the United Kingdom who receive more education through voluntary organisations in their communities than in schools and colleges. While the contribution to education of trade unions and co-operatives may have declined, thousands of Asians and Afro-Caribbeans receive desperately needed education in their places of worship. Along with many working class whites they perceive academic courses in sixth forms, and vocational courses in colleges, as largely irrelevant to their needs. Significant numbers fall into the category, identified in ALBSU and other research, whose members lack the basic skills necessary to undertake the training leading to recognised qualifications offered by further education colleges.

One of the most powerful statements on the limitation of vocationalism is Tawney's response to the Federation of British Industries 1918 state of policy (printed in *The Daily News*, 14 February 1918):

> stripped of its decent draperies of convention, what it means is that education is to be used, not to enable human beings to become themselves through the development of their personalities, not to strengthen the spirit of social solidarity, not to prepare men for the better service of their fellows, nor to raise the general level of society; but to create a new commercial aristocracy, based on the selection of the more promising children of working class parents from the vulgar mass, who are fit only to serve as the cannon-fodder of capitalists' industry.

The objectives identified by Tawney as being missing are equally absent from the government's education and training policies.   Apart from any issues of values or social objectives, the narrow vocational emphasis is a disaster because it is incapable of raising participation to the level necessary to reach national education and training targets.   In this sense narrow vocationalism, designed to serve the economy, hinders economic development and re-generation.   The greater emphasis on basic skills in more recent government publications, for example the 1996 *Competitiveness* white paper *Creating the Enterprise Centre of Europe*, is conceived as a mechanical adjustment: there is no understanding of the principles informing the European Year of Lifelong Learning, which as the Department for Education and Employment response indicates, the UK government regards as of only marginal importance.

The basic principle is that education is primarily for the development of the individual as a member of his/her community in a democratic society. Education for personal development has always been accepted for the elite in sixth forms and universities and there is no reason why the policy should be different for anyone else.   As well as being sound in principle, and the only means of creating equal opportunities, enabling all citizens to pursue education to the full realisation of their potential is necessary to develop the skills the economy requires.   Unless they start working life with a reasonable level of education, people will be unable to cope with change and the re-training it demands.

Community education recognises that workers are people, and that citizens better prepared for life are better prepared for work.   As Eric Robinson (ex Director of Lancashire Polytechnic and author of *The New Polytechnics* Pengium, 1968)) puts it:

> Everybody needs education and everybody needs training.   We must reject the nonsense that the superior people need education and the inferior people need training.   Along with this we must reject the idea that employers or the Department of Employment have a bigger role in the education of the inferior people than in the education of the superior people.

In *Labour and Education* (1990) Robinson draws attention to two of the priorities which must characterise an alternative (i.e. to the meritocratic) education and training service.   The first is the re-establishment of democracy at all levels:

Re-establishing democracy in education is a vital and integral part of re-establishing democracy generally and should not be considered in isolation.

This implies placing emphasis on, and directing resources to, social and community education, which are completely ignored in most training schemes, even when there is day release.

The *Penguin English Dictionary* defines "community" as meaning

(i)   *a society of people linked together by common conditions of life;*

(ii)   *organised under one authority;*

(iii)   *all members of a state, the public;*

(iv)   *ownership in common.*

It is the first and fourth of these which are relevant to colleges. An understanding of students' "common conditions of life" is essential to the development of relevant curriculum. The conditions of life of the majority who have succeeded at GCE A level and in higher education are not the same as experienced by people living on an estate in Bilston or Hackney where 50 per cent are unemployed. Developing relevant curriculum depends on recognition that the day-to-day experiences of the unemployed create stronger bonds than anything the academic and vocational traditions can nurture.

The obvious interpretation of "ownership in common" is a reminder that co-operative ownership is little developed in the UK as compared, for example, with France. It is also a reminder that educational progress and achievement is assisted by a sense of ownership about curriculum and the colleges which offer it. Consider how parents, through parents' associations, *own* sixth forms; middle-class adults students *own* their classes; industrialists, through advisory committees, *own* the courses offered to their employees. The unemployed with no stake of this kind are likely to regard education and training as belonging to *them*, like the factory where they used to work. They lost their jobs when the factory was closed - by *them*.

48   Community colleges and educating the community

There is a message here for colleges that would be community. It is not sufficient to assume that open access is a matter of opportunities for all to take existing academic and (or) vocational courses. And to take the view that the problem is that traditional qualifications are too difficult misses the point. They lack relevance and appeal because they relate to limited areas of human experience and operate in an ambience alien to out-of-work working-class people. GCE A levels assume a cultural environment unknown to most working class people, while vocational programmes are organised on the assumption that their students are in employment.

Education, like charity, begins at home. Society is made up of communities, each of which acquires shape and cohesion from shared experiences and the cultural traditions inherited. Although their values are not all positive, and they should not be idealised, communities are where many people acquire the education which enables them to survive. Although, to some degree, educationalists can become aware of people's traditions by involvement in their communities, the strongest influence on curriculum must inevitably be through participation in its development by the people themselves when they become students. This is what negotiated curriculum and student-centred learning is about, while the learner's involvement is a key element in a democratic system of further education.

The learning experiences of people in communities are not recognised by government, or the educational establishment, as *education* or *training* but as *leisure*, with the implication that they have little value or relevance to the important job of education and training people for work in the 1990s. Yet education is not, and never has been, confined to what occurs in schools, colleges, universities: it is a process by which individual personalities grow, develop, and learn to cope with all aspects of the world in which they live. Building curriculum on the experience of people in their communities is the community college alternative to the 1992 Further and Higher Education Act's imposition of academic and vocational traditions.

---

[1] Secretary at the Department of Science and Art (1850)

Chapter Four

Equal opportunities and quangocracy

Equal opportunities and community education

Under LEA control most colleges had formulated equal opportunities policies, while pressure by elected members for improved, or new, education and training for women, the disabled, ethnic minorities, was not uncommon. One effect of incorporation, indeed one of the government's reasons for it, was to remove this democratic influence. Awareness of the importance of equal opportunities was hardly discernible in the white paper *Education and Training for the 21st Century* and it did not feature prominently in the debates leading up to the 1992 Act. The notable exception was the debate on the Lords' Amendment, accepted by the government, on support for students with learning difficulties. Apart from meeting statutory requirements, and a few tentative (but very welcome) steps in the new funding methodology introduced in 1994, the FEFC has been largely silent on equal opportunities.

The concern is that neither the government nor FEFC recognise that without a high profile equal opportunities policy, with targeting of groups denied access, there is no chance that there will be sufficient participation to reach national education and training targets. The at best neutrality, on equal opportunities principles is accompanied by the virtual exclusion of a community education curriculum which, as already described, is the only means of access for many working class people, including substantial numbers of ethnic minorities.

At a seminar for leaders from the South African homelands in Johannesburg in 1996, there was a request for a definition of curriculum for community colleges: the simple two word reply, *the community*, was recognised and understood immediately. The response to this kind of answer by traditional educators in the UK is mystification, bewilderment and intellectual pity for those who proclaim it. Yet, unless the point of departure for community education is the experiences of people in their communities, there is no chance of creating access to further education and training for the millions currently denied it. The basis for lifelong learning is the learning in the life to date, not the formal teaching of basic skills, or assessment of competence in relation to practical tasks. Improvement of basic skills was recognised as a major challenge following the assessment of recruits to the services during the First and Second World Wars, a major reason for the 1918 and 1944 Education Acts. But as the memory of war faded it became apparent that there was no commitment to find the resources required.

The primary purpose of education in a democracy is to prepare people for citizenship by providing the foundation for lifelong learning. This is also the best preparation for work and re-training, not an alternative to it. The Joseph Rowntree Foundation sponsored report (February 1996) on unemployment is severely critical of job specific vocational training, arguing that the development of personal skills such as initiative and flexibility are not only more relevant for the individual but also to the requirements for jobs in the 1990s. The Major government's third *Competitiveness* white paper, *Creating the Enterprise Centre of Europe* (1996), goes no further than *The government will carry out a fundamental review of its policies for basic skills, assess all sectors and stages of education.* The refusal to base education and training programmes on where people are, rather than where vocationalists judge they should be, is the crucial weakness of the curriculum in the United Kingdom, including a great deal of further education provision.

As already recorded, the extent to which the Department for Education and Employment is out of touch is illustrated by its failure to respond with any enthusiasm to the European Year of Lifelong Learning. Its consultative paper (DfEE, SC, WO, 1995) confirms that vocationalism continues to be dominant, with adult community education regarded as on the margins and relevant to only a minority. Education in the community is, in fact, the most relevant form for young people under 18 currently excluded and for the majority of working class adults. Yet the impression given by the DfEE is that the only action likely to be taken would be for vocational purposes.. The only means of acquiring resources from the UK government for community education is to accredit it as vocational in compliance with the 1992 Act and apply for funding from the Further Education Funding Council. The experience in adult and community education services since 1993 is that there are people who are unwilling to join classes if accreditation is compulsory.

This is in sharp contrast to the approach to curriculum in USA community colleges, where the emphasis is on personal development and progression.

Nearer home, the message of the European Year of Lifelong Learning is recognition that vocationalism is irrelevant for millions of people; notably the estimated 25 million unemployed in the European Union's 15 states. As illustrated in the previous chapter, the main purpose of the white paper _Teaching and Learning: Towards the Learning Society_ is to draw attention to the teenagers and adults excluded from the high technology driven information society. The central question it poses is _How can those people pushed out of the mainstream, or those on the brink of exclusion, be re-integrated into society?_. If the numbers on the _brink of exclusion_ are added to the unemployed, the reference is to as much as one third of the population in some countries.

Encouragingly for community education, the solutions offered by the white paper are all anti-vocational and implicitly reject the academic approach to curriculum. Top down accreditation, which requires students' conformity to arbitrary criteria unrelated to their experiences, is rejected because it ignores skills acquired in communities - _skills not necessarily acquired by a paper qualification_. The recommendation is that the accreditation of prior experiential learning (APEL) should be followed by a scheme which _allows for an assessment of people's qualifications throughout their lives_. The case is not only for APEL at the point of entry but for an accreditation of prior experiential learning approach to assessment processes. The importance of this for community education is that it envisages opportunities for all to acquire recognition of what they know and what they can do. It is a process designed to break the link between quality and exclusiveness: the _knowledge_ recognised and accredited is what people have, not what elitist traditionalists deem they should have.

The other recommendations of the European white paper point towards the integration of education, training, community/economic re-generation and development. The limited success of European funded training projects in combating exclusion and creating jobs is privately recognised in Brussels and implicitly accepted in documents currently being issued by the Commission. Criteria for project approval now include expectations diametrically opposed to the obsessive vocationalism of the UK government: community participation, lifelong learning, personal development. They also include a requirement to assess the number of jobs likely to result from projects. The recognition that curriculum does not have to be narrowly vocational to prepare for jobs is an enormous advance on the position of the UK government.

The ex-polytechnics met and exceeded their student targets and there has been rapid growth in further education in recent years. Despite the government's commitment to vocationalism there has been progress on the accreditation front, especially where progressive universities, usually the former polytechnics, have supported Open College Network access federations to develop alternatives to the GCE A level and the NVQ routes to higher education.   In addition, there are university/college partnerships with a more relevant policy on assessment, including the assessment of prior learning which implies recognition that open access requires that the system should adapt to the needs of students,   rather than the traditional requirement that individuals adapt to the system.

The UK is well down the league (35th in 1995) for the participation rate in education and training, a problem for the economy which the National Targets for Education and Training (NTET) are designed to address.   Progress towards these targets to date is not encouraging, yet there is a growing belief that they are too modest by international standards. Although the rate of staying on at 16 increased steadily up to 1993, the 1995 figures indicate a falling back (BCCS, 1996). Even more serious is the low number staying on to 18: the UK was placed third from bottom of the world league table published by the Organisation for Economic Co-operation and Development (OECD) in 1996. Even worse news was that other countries were increasing their staying on rates faster than the UK. The majority of countries in the OECD report have a staying on to 18 rate of 75 per cent - 100 per cent, typically almost twice that of the UK.

In reality, the support from universities for a progressive approach to accreditation and assessment is not widespread, either in the number of universities involved, or in the contributions of departments of the involved universities. Equal partnerships with community colleges where a wide range of community education is accredited are the exception rather than the rule. In the majority of cases, even the colleges themselves have a minority of staff involved in, and committed to, open access community education.   Their management and administrative structures are not supportive of the control and development of curriculum at community level.   Indeed, establishing such a structure is extremely difficult given the outside pressures from the Further Education Funding Council, auditors, examining bodies. The growing control of colleges from the centre, with the regular issue of regulations to eat away discretion at local level, is making it more and more difficult to obtain funding for open access education and training in the community.

Another reason open access, equal opportunities, community education policies, designed to educate and train all citizens, are not implemented is that only a minority of managers and staff in education are committed to them. The commitment to meritocracy persists, with priority for academic and vocational traditions, not the experiences of people living in their communities. The result is often watered down A levels or vocational qualifications; modifications to the system to take some elements of community education into account rather than a building from the community base.

A growing number of colleges are recognising that meeting their own and national targets depends on reaching out and providing opportunities in communities, preferably in partnership with community organisations. The opportunity for franchising arrangements 1994/96 encouraged colleges to establish positive community partnerships and it appeared for a time that the needs of the disadvantaged would be given a higher priority. Then along came the FEFC juggernaut with bureaucratic requirements, published retrospectively, to restrict equal opportunities provision. This was the most blatant demonstration that democratically expressed needs of communities for education and training counted for nothing. When colleges protested that a twenty page contract was not the means towards increasing participation, the reply was that if colleges and community organisations did not conform they would lose their funding.

Equal opportunities and quangocracy

When the government established its national education and training targets, and created a further education sector funded and policed by the FEFC, it was apparent that raising the participation rate depended on making inroads into the neglected half. Yet, as already demonstrated, the 1992 Further and Higher Education Act prevented the FEFC from funding adult non-vocational and community education - education without the primary aim of a recognised vocational qualification on the Department for Education and Employment's list (Schedule II of the 1992 Act - see previous chapter). But, because it quickly became obvious that the recognised qualifications objective made no sense whatsoever for people with special educational needs, this area was excluded from the requirement. To the extent that it could be demonstrated that it provided the basic skills support needed by students with major learning difficulties, community education became fundable. But the constant threat that programmes leading to college certificates would be funded for only a minimum period revealed an ignorance of the nature and extent of the support necessary for some of these students.

Ironically, in this context, in 1994 a new system of funding was introduced, its main objective to encourage participation - for example by funding tuition fees for the unemployed and supporting a more comprehensive information, advice and guidance service. Equally significant in terms of opportunities is what is called *the Demand Led Element* which, albeit at a rate less than half the standard unit value, funds growth at whatever level. At first it appeared that there would be a more equitable approach to funding which, along with the Demand Led Element (DLE), would enable colleges to extend access, and that colleges committed to equal opportunities and increasing participation would benefit. In reality, the improvement was only marginal, mainly because colleges with large growth were compelled to fund most of it at the lower rate. Factors, such as the participation rate in a college's locality, were not taken into account in funding allocations.

Franchising, mainly to colleges of further education, had played an important part in the rapid growth of higher education after the polytechnics were established. Some colleges had a strong tradition of providing education in the community on an outreach basis and on employers' premises. The pressure for growth after 1992 encouraged franchising on a large scale, publicly supported by FEFC leaders, who were present when Handsworth College launched its community franchising strategy. About a year later, Handsworth received a critical report on its community franchising from FEFC inspectors.

A four year inspection cycle for colleges had been determined shortly after incorporation in 1993 and the criteria, set down in an FEFC circular, indicated that colleges would be assessed in terms of their own objectives. In reality, inspectors had a check list based on traditional further education criteria, which, unsurprisingly, proved totally inadequate when applied to community education as in the Handsworth case. When they visited Bilston in 1994, some inspectors were honest enough to admit that the criteria did not fit the college, although this did not prevent the award of grades in strict accordance with the standard check list. They were, however, embarrassed when, independently, college management and members of the corporation drew attention to some of the absurdities of trying to apply to a community college the mechanistic criteria based on traditional further education practice.

It is no criticism of the inspectors, who operated with the highest level of professionalism, that they could not do an impossible job. When the nature of the impossibility became evident during the first preparatory visit, the inspector in charge decided not to include Bilston in the first year inspection programme: a few days later he was overruled and the inspection took place. The problem - that the check list was not applicable to education in the community - was solved by ignoring most of the community education. The failure to evaluate outreach programmes in their context, or to focus on the education and training needs of the outreach students, is indicative of the FEFC's low priority for equal opportunities issues, a direct consequence of the 1992 Act's exclusion of adult non-vocational and community education.

Despite identifying with the Handsworth strategy, the FEFC provided no clear guidance on franchising. When colleges not used to operating in community partnerships became involved, it was hardly surprising that circumstances arose which suggested misappropriation of funds, with the appearance, or more accurately non-appearance, of phantom students. Franchising with FEFC funding started in 1993 and it was May 1996 before the Council issued its model contract, along with a circular which implied that the new *rules* would together be backdated, thus threatening to make some franchise students ineligible for funding. This unilateral change to contracts with colleges was becoming common by 1996: for example on Demand Led Element payments as already mentioned. In May 1995 the FEFC signed funding agreements with colleges stating that the Demand Led Element payments would be made in February, April, July: a few months later it issued a circular stating that growth up to 30 per cent only would be paid on the specified dates.

By 1996 the further education sector was in deep crisis, with the FEFC floundering hopelessly and concentrating on ensuring that where there was difficulty, as with Wilmorton, the blame would fall on colleges. Some institutions were facing bankruptcy, with mass redundancies the only means of escape but not necessarily a guarantee of escape. The situation was so dire that even colleges which had met all their targets were compelled to lay off staff. There was no equal treatment: colleges in middle class areas received higher levels of funding than areas with high unemployment, while there were wide variations in funding for colleges with very similar catchment areas. As an example, in 1996/97 Bilston received £16.85 per unit of funding, while a neighbouring college, serving a very similar area, received £22.71. Had Bilston been funded at the same level as the other college, its 1996/97 budget would have been £4½ million greater.

These figures demonstrate the failure of the FEFC's policy of convergence to equalise funding. The policy failed because it was based on the wishful thinking that government funding would permit a levelling up rather than a requirement for the more highly funded colleges to reduce their unit costs dramatically. Nobody would have argued that the generously funded colleges should have had their budgets reduced in the first year but if the FEFC had been committed to equality it would have ensured convergence in three years at maximum. Also, because the Council did not fund the poorly funded colleges at the full rate the following year for the students they recruited above target, there were cases where the unit of funding for colleges with a low unit of resource reduced more rapidly than that of colleges with a high level of funding.

As described in Chapter Two, the treatment of colleges which received funding from Europe, typically for unemployed and disabled students, did not assist equal opportunities. The purpose of the funding, for example under Objective II and Objective III categories of the European Social Fund, is to enhance provision for the disadvantaged. The blunt use of a formula to deduct from college budgets the amount of European grant received meant that the efforts of obtaining the funding brought no significant benefit. The colleges involved were often those which received a lower than average level of FEFC funding.

As these facts demonstrate the situation was both inequitable and unreasonable. Although there was a great deal of propaganda about openness and fairness, the FEFC had no mechanism for negotiation on any of these issues: when corporations attempted to raise questions, as democratically requested by their communities, they were ignored. The Council applied its systems mechanistically and when disagreements arose had no means of resolving them. One consequence was that disputes dragged on for years, at great public expense, with small prospect of resolution. By 1996, it was clear that in the event of dispute it was cheaper to take court action than to attempt to resolve differences by discussion with the FEFC.

Equal opportunities through community education : the FEFC's response

Supported by a progressive Director of Education, Bilston established a mechanism for funding community education following the 1988 Education

Reform Act. This mechanism was explained to a number of FEFC officers 1992/94 and it was agreed that, to the extent that it created access to courses leading to recognised qualifications, it could be included in the 1993/94 returns for funding purposes. The mechanism was audited by the college's internal auditors in 1994, which resulted in recommendations for some tidying up but there was an acceptance that the mechanism was basically sound.

During the same year, a large firm of auditors, acting on behalf of the FEFC, refused to audit the community education mechanism and gave the college a low grade because of it. When representations were made the auditors refused to alter their position and referred the matter to the FEFC on the grounds that the Council's brief determined the audit position. Three years later the position remained unresolved. The equal opportunities effect was that education in the community for working class people, the majority of whom in this particular case were Afro-Caribbeans or Asians, or people with special educational needs, was not funded.

Ironically, the refusal to fund 1993/94 related to the area which was partly addressed by the new funding methodology from 1994. Part, but not all, of the 1993/94 claim was for student advice and counselling, now covered by entry unit funding. The mechanistic system, however, continues to discriminate against colleges which offer community education beyond the further education norm. There are severe financial disadvantages where enrolment is all the year round rather than concentrated in the September - December period because the Council insists on paying all colleges on the basis of a standard enrolment profile. All the year round enrolment, which implies shorter rather than longer student programmes, is a feature of access provision for working-class people.

The paragraphs in this section will, quite sensibly, be skipped by many readers because they are technical and boring, and it is entirely predictable that the FEFC, and well-off colleges in middle-class areas, will dismiss them as parochial special pleading. They are here to demonstrate that the administrative process related to funding is tedious in the extreme, not least because at no point does it include consideration of the education and training of people. There is no place in the system where equal opportunities questions can be addressed seriously, while expenditure is incurred producing computer disks and on auditing and re-auditing.

The mechanistic system excludes all opportunity for democratic input. As will be demonstrated in the last chapter, the concentration of all power and decision-making at the centre is the antithesis of a democratic, equal opportunities approach to organisation. The only consolation (and it is no consolation to people who have been denied access), is that by Stalinistic centralisation of power, obsession with regulations and auditing, unilateral breach of agreements with colleges, bullying of small quangos (corporations) into submission, the FEFC has played into the hands of the opponents of quangocracy.

Chapter Five

Community college strategy and management: the Bilston Consortium

Community colleges before 1984

As described in Chapter Three, community colleges in England before 1984 were school based, a combination of activities under schools regulations for pre sixteens and further education regulations for over sixteens and adults. Well-known examples are the Cambridge village colleges and the Leicestershire community colleges: in other areas, although *community schools* was a more usual term, the programmes were much the same, with partnerships between schools and LEA adult education services a common model. Because school and adult activities were normally planned separately, there were conflicts between school and adult education staff on the use of accommodation and equipment. In some cases, the head of the school was in overall charge: in others there was a separate head for adult education who reported directly to the governors and the LEA.

The use of school buildings for adult, youth, community activities is clearly a sensible policy, especially in rural areas where the nearest college may be 10 or 20 miles. Less sensible is the separate planning of adult education in schools and colleges. Competition has been incited by incorporating colleges while leaving LEAs with adult (non-vocational, community) education and by changing regulations to enable schools to offer programmes for adults. In some areas there are partnerships - schools, LEAs, colleges, or two of the three: in other areas there is fierce competition resulting in a waste of scarce resources on marketing and small classes. LEAs no longer have powers to do anything about this and neither does any other agency: partnerships to agree an overall strategy are the exception.

Historically, some further education colleges offered adult and community education, usually in rural areas, but others, especially in urban areas, concentrated on full-time courses for school leavers and/or vocational studies for part-time day students released from work. They regarded themselves as *further education* or *technical* rather than *community* colleges. Providing a service for school leavers and students released from work were the priorities, even where there was involvement with adult non-vocational programmes. Most lecturers were drawn from schools or industry, bringing experience of the academic or vocational traditions. Where colleges were the providers of adult and community education, these were usually in separate departments or faculties, and sometimes in separate buildings.

The pattern started to change in the late 1970s as unemployment increased and persisted. More students enrolled as individuals - from the community rather than from a school or an employer. Colleges also became involved in youth and adult training schemes funded from the Department for Employment: there were YTS community projects and, later, the community programmes for adults. The word *community* denoted that the projects were based on voluntary organisations in the community, yet they were vocational in objectives and curriculum content. The schemes gave a harder edge to the term *community* and in some cases non-vocational and community activity was vocationalised and funded by the Department of Employment, directly or through one of its agencies. But, although more colleges became involved with their communities as a result of projects to counter unemployment, few regarded this as their main function or considered themselves to be community colleges.

As described in Chapter Three, the best known community colleges, not based on schools and offering programmes for adults as their main function, are in the USA. Their work became better known in England in the 1980s, largely from study tours for English principals organised by the Further Education Staff College. The participation rate of adults was impressive and there was a growing awareness that it needed to be emulated here. Equally impressive was the high regard for community colleges from USA citizens and political leaders. In comparison, United Kingdom further education colleges were the poor relations of the education system,hardly recognised in Whitehall or Westminster.

Bilston Community College

Bilston's claim to be the first community college in England under further education regulations has already been recorded. Before 1984 there were two colleges in Bilston: a college of further education suffering from the decline in the engineering industry, and a sixth form college created to placate grammar school parents, who did not want their offspring to mix with people in dirty overalls in further education. The setting up of the sixth form college in 1975, when a boys' and a girls' grammar school became an 11-16 comprehensive, was unnecessary and wasteful. It was never intended to have more than 300 students studying GCEs, a number which could have been easily accommodated by the further education college.

The pressure for change came from the community. Unemployed people, many of whom had been redundant when the British Steelworks closed in 1979, were incensed that they were offered no relevant training when large sums were wasted on small GCE A level groups and half-empty engineering workshops. They became even more incensed when told they could not enrol on craft classes where there were vacancies *because they were unemployed.* The conclusion was that neither institution was capable of changing to meet the needs of the locality. Both were closed and Bilston Community College opened, with a brief to modernise and improve the quality of traditional courses; develop curriculum for school leavers excluded by the academic and vocational traditions; expand provision for adults, especially the unqualified and unemployed.

Because the college was established following pressure from the community, including the Member of Parliament (Bob Edwards) and local councillors, it was opposed from the outset by the majority of the local education authority officers. What they disliked in particular was the co-operation of members of the community, councillors, the MP, trade unions, college managers, who worked and campaigned together as the Bilston Friends of Open Education. Issues were discussed in the open, instead of behind closed doors, while officers were obliged to justify their decisions.   There was strong resistance to democratic decision-making beyond the casting of a vote for a councillor every three or four years.   Other local authority departments (social services, economic development) were more supportive, especially in partnership on projects for the unemployed and disabled.

In view of later developments at Bilston, it is significant that one of the strongest supporters was Bob Edwards, the best known internationalist in parliament at the time, with his strong commitment to open access, equal opportunities, community education. His work was carried on by his successor Dennis Turner, who as a local councillor chaired the Bilston Friends of Open Education and was a member of the new college's governing body. Another committed supporter was Terry Pitt, the Member of the European Parliament, who assisted in acquiring European funding, especially for the unemployed and disabled. After his tragic early death, support was continued by his successor, John Bird, and then by Simon Murphy, the current MEP.

The key to understanding Bilston Community College, however, is not the involvement of well-known public figures but the commitment and contributions of members of the community and their leaders. These included the members of the Springvale Co-operative, who pooled their redundancy money and took over the social club when British Steel closed, and trade unionists and other community leaders too numerous to record. They are represented by the late Gilbert Mould, Frank Venton, Jack Collingswood, Bert Turner, Aaron Haynes, Mel Chevannes, Gillian Carver, John Kyte (first chair of governors) and Alan Millington, the current chair of the corporation.

These are the descendants of Tawney's *humble men and women* of the nineteenth century. Their commitment is to education and training for all, with priority for creating access in the community for working-class people. In the area which Bilston serves this includes Afro-Caribbean and Asian citizens, many of whom have had a poor deal at school. Conflict with the LEA was frequently on projects with specific equal opportunities objectives, such as women into construction and programmes of Asian languages for pupils in schools.

By rejecting elitism and developing community education, the college, not unexpectedly, met opposition from the establishment. This conflict put commitment to open access to the test and the college survived because the leaders named above, and supporters too numerous to name, never wavered. Others, including some councillors, proved fair weather friends, partly because they could not accept that, without rejecting the values of the elitist establishment and developing community education, it was impossible to create access for the majority of working-class people. Some were also unnerved by the frequent scare stories that the college was financially unsound and might collapse, stories which were communicated to the FEFC on incorporation.

The record shows persistent opposition by the LEA, illustrated by a refusal to provide any mainstream increase in funding over the period 1984/93, even though student enrolment more than trebled. Although there was also opposition to the college raising funding from other sources, this did not prevent substantial income, mainly from the European Social Fund, through support of local councillors able to bypass the education department. The strength of the LEA opposition is demonstrated by a refusal to negotiate on disputed budget matters when the college became independent in 1993. The Council decided on court action rather than negotiation, even though legal costs are likely to be higher than the claim of £345,000 (with a college counter-claim of over £2 million).

There was never any suggestion that the college failed to implement the open access policies laid down by the LEA. The opposition arose because these policies were pursued by involving members of the community in decision-making. The LEA opposition increased with the number of working-class people enrolled, partly because this illustrated the failure to escape from elitist provision in other parts of the Borough: students in sixth forms were funded at a much higher level than college students. Bilston was able to develop as a community college, despite this opposition, because the needs and demands of the community were fully supported by the governing body. In general, this included the support of governors who were also members of the Borough Council, although there were occasions when some councillors took one line as governors, another on the LEA education committee. There was no open challenge to the strategy and policies but persistent attempts to undermine college management by the administration. This included a refusal to issue contracts to staff properly appointed by the governors (until the law was invoked) and a failure, despite a committee decision, to establish a separate account for college cost recovery income, which was a legal requirement following the 1988 Education Reform Act.

The history of Bilston Community College illustrates that the education service, at national and local level, is controlled by elitists prepared to accept only modest extension of access for working-class people. Elitists are opposed to education for all working-class people in their communities, partly because embarrassing questions are raised about the distribution of resources. Despite all the pressure, and evidence of inequality, there was no means of persuading Wolverhampton officers to recommend to councillors that Bilston college students should be funded at the same level as sixth formers, or students elsewhere in the borough.

From the outset, Bilston Community College pursued a policy of providing education through community partnerships, as reflected in the vision statement:

Bilston Community College aims to be the best College for open access, equal opportunities **through** meeting individual education and training needs and aspirations **largely by** partnerships with other providers, employers, the community.

The policy is involvement with partners on an equal basis, with shared decision-making. A range of different types of constitutions cover the partnerships, including co-operatives and companies limited by shares. This enables the participation of a wider range of people in strategy, planning, management than the limited number who serve on the governors (corporation). Also, companies and co-operatives are able to apply for funds not available to corporations and there are tax benefits. Local authority opposition meant that it took five years to establish a company, Stowlawn Ltd, which had just completed its first full financial year on incorporation in 1993: another company, Bilston (E.O.&C.) Training Ltd, was just starting to trade.

The key factor is that the co-operatives and companies were established to meet community need (for education, training, job creation) by involving staff, management, members of the community, in decision-making. Democratic participation is not merely a matter of formal elections and committee meetings but an essential process for ensuring that the curriculum developed, and the way in which it is organised, is relevant to students. It was an enormous advantage to Bilston in 1984 that strategy and policies were fully discussed by the Bilston Friends of Open Education, and that a workers' co-operative was fully represented. The Springvale Co-operative, with around 100 affiliated community organisations, was the best possible means of involving members of the community in the college and the college in the community.

It is, perhaps, necessary to add that no member of the corporation, company board of directors, management, staff receives any benefit, financial or otherwise, from the companies. *Profits* are, by covenant, paid to a trust which exists to support the college's community education policies. Over the years since 1984 these companies and co-operatives have defended and developed community education, especially by raising large sums from Europe, currently over £3m per year. Surpluses from income generation activities have subsidised FEFC-funded and non-vocational work, typically by around £500,000 per year. Also, funding acquired by companies has enabled Bilston to develop international projects, with visitors from many parts of the world enriching the local culture and benefiting the local economy.

At an early stage it became apparent that the FEFC was concerned about the companies. Council officers could not conceive that they exist to benefit the community. This is perhaps excusable, even though the audited accounts show that income from sources other than the FEFC subsidised FEFC-funded work by £370,000 1993/94 and £470,000 1994/95. What is not excusable, and has damaged the community projects and hindered income generation, is the way the matter was dealt with by FEFC personnel. Apart from demonstrating that the Council's protestations of openness do not accord with its practices, the episode is further evidence of the negative attitude to community education described in the last chapter.

Community partnerships have always been central to Bilston's strategy, as described in detail in *Bilston College and its Community* (submitted to the FEFC in 1993 as part of a development plan) and in papers prepared for the inspectors. A discussion of the strategy would have been welcomed and could have prevented time-wasting and conflict 1993/95. There was no discussion but both internal and external auditors were asked questions about Bilston's college companies. No useful information resulted from the questions, mainly because auditors had been told that the companies were not involved with FEFC funding. The FEFC's concern appears to have resulted from a photograph of the chief executive drinking champagne, with the caption that one of Bilston's companies had imported 100 million (or some large figure) bottles from Russia.

A number of issues arise. If there was concern, why was the matter not raised with the college? There was no secret about the facts: the champagne had been purchased by a Russian businessman who asked Bilston to test the market. There was an understanding that, in the event of a profit, it would be shared. Second, even if Stowlawn Ltd had purchased the champagne, the FEFC had sufficient financial information to avoid any suggestion that it was bought with FEFC money. Third, it is not at all clear from the 1992 Act that it would have been illegal to use FEFC money, given that the project was part of an education and training project; although this would have been of questionable wisdom.

The situation rapidly degenerated into farce and provided light relief at corporation meetings, yet there were serious professional issues involved. An FEFC auditor suddenly appeared to carry out a *routine FEFC audit*. The only facts I can recall about a long discussion was that I was unable to produce my job description (because I did not have one) and that I was asked more or less the same questions as an inspector had asked a week earlier. There was no mention of champagne but the next day my finance director was asked about it. His reply - that only the chief executive had information about the champagne - must have suggested that it was purchased for my personal use for the auditor sought another urgent interview. There followed a two-hour meeting on company partnerships, every word of which appeared to be taken down. The only response was that the companies were subsidiaries of the corporation, with the implication that the (non) purchase of the champagne was a matter for the FEFC. The FEFC statement on subsidiary status was subsequently contradicted by the external auditors after some extensive research at companies' house.

The next surprise was that, when the auditor's report arrived, there was no reference to the champagne interview. By that time, another FEFC auditor had appeared and expressed the view that there was nothing improper about the champagne - it could, he opined, be payment for training. The decision at this stage was whether to present the auditor with a bottle of champagne or the college's book on community education: the latter was considered more appropriate. Another officer was delighted to accept a bottle but had to be provided with a bag because he was worried about being seen carrying it out of the college. There is probably no connection, but over a year later a story appeared in the *Times Educational Supplement* claiming that Bilston's champagne was undrinkable. Drinkable or not, there is every sign that it is immortal.

Despite frequent requests, the auditor's notes were never produced and neither, until two years later, was the final draft of the auditor's report There were rumours of discussions on trains and there was undoubtedly a dispute between the college's internal auditors and the FEFC. Members of the audit committee made frequent demands to see the report - undoubtedly for its entertainment value, as nobody believed it could make any contribution to improving the management or financial systems of the college. The internal auditors threatened to sue the FEFC - in letters they refused to copy to the college, although the FEFC did copy the replies.

This, much abbreviated, version of the champagne saga is at once tedious, hilarious, and a matter for serious concern. The first question which arises is why, in the first instance, the college was not asked for the facts. The response might, or might not, have justified an audit investigation but on the grounds of common sense, as well as normal standards of professionalism, this must be regarded as, at minimum, a serious error. The second question is why the matter was raised, indirectly, with the internal auditors, and directly with the finance director, but not with the chief executive. Thirdly, what has happened to the notes? The fact that they have not been included in a report, with an opportunity for comment, by the college, means that even the element of fairness of an official inquiry is missing.

Where this kind of *dispute* with the FEFC arises, there is no machinery for resolution - except the courts, and the legal path inevitably results in a further diversion from the primary task: the education and training of students. In the champagne case the exchange of letters and reports continued for two years and, as recorded in the previous chapter, the exchange of disks on the 1993/94 student returns covered a similar period. The total cost, in staff time, disks, meetings, opportunities lost, etc. is estimated as over £3million, far greater than the disputed sums, or the value of the champagne.

It is unlikely that there is a deliberate intention to destroy community colleges, although there are certainly those determined to *quang* them into conformity. The difficulties arise from a system which demands a level of conformity incompatible with responses to a wide variety of education and training needs. Responding speedily to diverse needs has been the strength of the further education system - a strength which will disappear to the extent that colleges are *quanged* into conformity. The problems described arose largely because the FEFC, and those associated with it, have a working knowledge of traditional further education but no significant experience of open access, community education for working-class people.

Bilston's response is to continue to argue the case and make the structural and management changes necessary to implement a community education strategy relevant to the 21st century. There is every confidence that developments over the next five years will demonstrate that it is the FEFC that is out of line. The emphasis on community, democracy, regionalisation by the European Commission is more important than is recognised by the UK government and its quangos. The conflicts and tensions between colleges and the FEFC are not caused by the way its officers operate, which is a symptom rather than a cause. This cause is a system incapable of taking into account the democratically expressed wishes of people in their communities.

The Bilston Consortium : development of the community college concept

Bilston Community College opened in 1984 in an area with one of the lowest education and training participation rates in the country and no prospect of a building programme. The priority - to extend education to the neglected half (the majority working class with substantial numbers of ethnic minorities) was never expected to receive positive support from elitist officers and administrators at local or national level. The confidence that the policies would succeed emanated from the knowledge of community commitment and support, including the support of the elected local and national representatives. Bilston Community College survived and developed because, throughout the years of difficulty and conflict, this support never faltered, a positive message, for colleges that would be community. Colleges, denied funding because they do not conform to traditional elitist patterns, can never become rich but, with community support, they can become strong.

It was evident that, however much efficient use improved (and there was room for improvement), existing buildings could accommodate expansion for, at most, two years. It was also recognised that many non-participants could not be persuaded to travel from their communities to college sites. Although the reasons are frequently financial, discouraging and alienating school experience also plays an important part. The solution, for reasons of both accommodation and student need, was to take education and training to the community. In practice, this meant acquiring whatever suitable buildings became available and establishing partnerships with community organisations, using their facilities. It was accepted from the outset that success depends on the involvement of community leaders, as equal partners, in organisation and development.

A number of old school buildings were acquired but the most important decision was to establish a partnership with Springvale Co-operative, as described earlier in this chapter. Unable to identify suitable education and training for the unemployed in the old colleges, the co-operative had set up a company, Springvale Training Ltd, to manage a youth training scheme (YTS) community project. Apart from the specific training offered, the co-operative and the company were committed to education and training for all. There was no policy difference and, because there was a commitment to quality and public service, the training element of the Springvale Co-operative was transferred to the new community college. Stowlawn Ltd was established to operate in the community context and take over the training function of Springvale Training Ltd. The Springvale Co-operative has, over the years, demonstrated a commitment to open access education not just to create opportunities for its own members, but also to support community links across the world - for example, in Eastern Europe and South Africa. For the development of Bilston Community College this has provided a positive antidote to the narrow vocationalism of government policies as administered through the FEFC.

Stowlawn Ltd was established to co-ordinate externally funded projects on behalf of the college, to generate income to finance community projects, and to encourage and extend democratic input to strategy and development. In accord with the principle of community participation, and a management policy of delegated responsibility, two other companies were established - to focus on equal opportunities generally in one case (Bilston (E.O.&C.) Training Ltd) and on projects, including job creation, for those with learning difficulties in the other (Semoon Ltd). Directors and managers work closely with members of the community, increasingly through partnerships with community-based organisations. The three company partnerships are the college's main agents in the community, which now includes the international community.

The companies are three of the largest partners, which now total over 150: employers and community organisations - local, regional, national and international. The growth of student numbers after 1994, particularly rapid at weekends as well as through partnerships, made it necessary to review existing organisation, management, administrative structures. The review was necessary to ensure efficient operation on all sites, maintain quality, and protect the arrangements for democratic participation evolved over the years. During the same period international work also expanded, making it necessary to review arrangements for co-ordination and management of projects overseas.

The primary consideration was how the resources available should be allocated and managed to assist the maximum number of people. It was concluded that funding were still biased towards traditional curriculum areas, when the greatest growth was in the community and in the college at non-traditional times, especially weekends. Internationally, projects tended to be managed on an ad-hoc basis and often separately from projects at Bilston, even when the curriculum was similar. The action taken in the re-structuring which followed the review included:

> (i)   reduction of teaching hours by extending student-based
>   learning in learning centres, and through open learning;
>
> (ii)   creation of new types of posts to provide learning support;
>
> (iii)   integration of local, regional, national, international
>   provision for curriculum development;
>
> (iv)   integration of education, training, economic development.

It was clear that the most urgent requirement was a new structure, the Bilston Consortium, accompanied by large-scale management and staff training and re-training, with the emphasis on project management, open learning curriculum, income generation. It was estimated that the resources released would permit at least 20 per cent growth in FEFC-funded work for two years, and it was planned that income generation from sources other than the FEFC would support expansion at a similar rate thereafter.

The Bilston Consortium

Establishing the Bilston Consortium required integration of the governance, strategy, management, administration of the college and the original partnership companies without in any way limiting their freedom to develop, especially in the community and internationally. The management core of the Consortium is

> Bilston Community College
> Bilston (E.O.&C.) Training Ltd
> Semoon Ltd
> Stowlawn Ltd

Other members for the purposes of strategy development, extension of community partnerships, integration of education and training with community and economic re-generation, are:

> The Bilston Community College Foundation
> The Black Country Partnership College
> The Open College of the Black Country
> The Springvale Co-operative

The Foundation is a registered charity, which raises funds for community education projects and to support individual students suffering hardship. Projects from the partnership companies' commercial activities are covenanted to the Foundation, with obvious tax advantages. The crucial role of the Springvale Co-operative has already been described and its existence is the main reason it has been possible to maintain and extend democratic participation since the college was incorporated. The Black Country Partnership College's brief is to co-ordinate, through partnerships, provision for 14 - 25 year olds throughout the Black Country, and, by operating on a regional basis, to maximise funding opportunities, especially from European sources.

The Open College of the Black Country was established in 1985 to co-ordinate and manage provision not funded by the LEA. Its brief includes initiating and developing courses and projects at non-traditional times and a development unit was established for this purpose in 1993. Because the demand was greater than expected, especially for vocational (FEFC funded) work, within two years it was enrolling over 10,000 students. Contrary to intention, the Open College of the Black Country found itself organising and developing curriculum, mainly because the traditional directorates were unable, in some cases unwilling, to operate at week-ends. The partnership companies, and the Open College of the Black Country, had each developed separately from the mainstream work of the college and it was clear that greater integration would mean a much more efficient use of resources.

The timing of the re-structuring to establish the Bilston Consortium was strongly influenced by the confirmation of year by year reduction of funding by the government and the expansion of projects overseas. Partnerships in South Africa and Eastern Europe demonstrated that, in many parts of the world, education and training can be resourced only if it is integrated with economic re-generation, principally to create jobs. It was equally apparent that, to a degree, the same applies to areas such as Bilston: European grants to assist students to acquire qualifications are of limited value without economic re-generation and the creation of jobs.

The Bilston Consortium is recognition that new models of governance, organisation, management are required for community colleges. In this case the network includes over 150 organisations, all in partnership with a member of the Consortium. The function of the core members of the Consortium is to ensure efficient management and operation on all sites, in England and internationally. Strategy is negotiated and agreed with each of the partners and it is the responsibility of members of the Consortium to consult with community and employer partners and to keep them informed of developments. The annual plan for each is agreed and monitored by management groups which serve the whole Consortium. Members of the community serve on the governing bodies of each (corporation, boards of directors), as do managers and staff of the college. The total available experience and expertise is now more easily available to members of the Consortium. This assists the expansion of international work, as compared with previous arrangements when it was often difficult for Stowlawn Ltd, for example, to identify and acquire the necessary expertise from the college.

Operation as a consortium extends opportunities to acquire funding from external sources. Internationally, communities can be linked to communities, employers to employers, as well as colleges to colleges. Visitors from Russia, South Africa, Poland are always welcomed at the Springvale Co-operative Club, which continues to play a vital part in the development of strategy, as do many other organisations, for example, those representing ethnic minorities, operating in partnership with the college or a company. The overall structure, considered to be a natural development for community colleges, is as below. Although all community partners have access to the resources of the whole Consortium, for management and administrative purposes each has an agreement with a core member.

The Bilston Consortium and Partners

Members: strategy and management

Bilston Community College (5 colleges)
Bilston Community College Foundation
Bilston Equal Opportunities and Conferences Ltd
Black Country Partnership College
Springvale Co-operative
Open College of the Black Country
Semoon Ltd
Stowlawn Ltd

Associated partners (examples)

Bilston Education Centre (BCC)
Bilston Town Football Club (Stowlawn Ltd)
Black Education Consortium (Bilston EO & C Ltd)
British College of Banking and Finance, Moscow (Stowlawn Ltd)
Citizens of the Third Age Network (Semoon Ltd)
Over 100 Community Clubs (Springvale)
Ryton Hall Management Services (Stowlawn Ltd)
The London Consortium (BCC)

The re-structuring which created the Consortium also required major changes in the college. One hundred and twenty posts were made redundant and three directorates, concerned primarily with the traditional further education curriculum, were closed down. Five new curriculum divisions were created, each, on average, intended to enrol ten to twenty thousand students and to contribute to implementing Consortium strategy. Divisions are now called *colleges* and the heads have the same degree of management autonomy as the managing directors of the companies. The territory of executive managers is the Consortium and their targets the Consortium's targets. The colleges are expected to operate through a series of partnerships - local, regional, national, international.

Management is based on the action learning principles of Professor Reg Revans, who visited Bilston on a number of occasions in the 70s and 80s (when he was in his 70s and 80s). His conviction that people in communities must solve their own problems is increasingly recognised as the only way forward in areas of industrial decline ignored by government and major commercial investors. Considered internationally, this recognition applies to where a half to two thirds of the world population lives. The fact that this management policy works has been demonstrated by the achievements of outreach centres, especially the British College of Banking and Finance in Moscow. The major requirements in applying it throughout the Consortium, nationally and internationally, is investment in management and staff re-training.

The Consortium, and the Revans' policy on management, are responses to the demand for rapid expansion of education and training in communities. The community college of the future will be a network of organisations, operating in partnerships and unconstrained by geography and distance. For many adults access must be created in their communities, and in any case there will be no large scale investment from government sources in buildings and equipment. In the short term there is unlikely to be substantial funding available for investment in new technology, which obviously has potential for linking centres of learning, and for the development of curriculum.

The USA community colleges were a response to community need and demand when investment was available on a scale unlikely to occur elsewhere. For some of the same reasons as at Bilston, their development for the 21st century will have a greater outreach emphasis. In South Africa and under-developed countries, where there are enormous demands for basic education, the only option is community colleges operating on a network of sites. Introducing mass adult education is possible only by creating colleges based on schools and existing community organisations. Their revenue income will depend almost entirely on grants and economic re-generation, an issue to which we shall return in the next chapter.

An emphasis on democracy has always characterised USA community colleges. Democracy is a requirement of the African National Congress as it struggles to build a new, multi-racial society and an objective of East and Central European states. Although in the UK democracy has had a low priority since the 1992 Further and Higher Education Act, it has a much higher priority in the European Union and is a requirement for the allocation of European structural funds, which also place an emphasis on job creation. Re-establishing democracy in colleges in England can be given impetus by international links, as has been demonstrated by the Bilston Consortium's partnership with the Community Colleges Association of South Africa. This is another justification for international partnerships.

Chapter Six

The international challenge and economic re-generation

India in Bilston and Bilston in Moscow

Colleges with black students have always been conscious of the cultures of other countries, in Bilston's case the countries of Middle Asia, the Caribbean, Africa. One of the disappointments of the last forty years is the insistence on regarding the educational needs of Asians and Afro-Caribbeans as problems rather than opportunities for cultural enrichment. What Christopher Caudwell (1938) called the dying cultures of the West could have been re-vitalised by a more positive response to cultural diversity. Instead, to quote Paul Robeson, *Western man seems to have gained more and more abstraction at the expense of his creative faculties* (Robeson, in Hyams, 1963). Vocationalisation is not only the wrong response to the education and training needs of the economy: its most serious offence is the denial of opportunities for people to develop their creative potential. In Robeson's words:

> To understand this you need to remember that by 'creative ability' one means something more than the capacity of a few individuals to paint, to write, or to make music. That is simply the supreme development of a quality that exists in the make-up of every human being. The whole problem of living can never be understood until the world recognises that artists are not a race apart. Every man has some element of the artist in him, and if this is pulled up by the roots he becomes suicidal and dies.

There are many reasons for the rejection of other cultures, including the belief in white superiority, most blatant during the apartheid period in South Africa. It is now recognised that the notion of black inferiority has no basis in reality and that some African music, for example, has subtleties of rhythm far finer than anything achieved by a Western composer. Awareness that the majority of working class people have been denied the chance to realise their creative potential is the case for open access, equal opportunities, community education.

A vocational, as opposed to a lifelong learning, approach to education can never be genuinely open access because it focuses on too limited a range of abilities and skills.

The black townships of South Africa have little further education and in the country as a whole there are over 15 million adults lacking basic skills. Yet the embryonic community colleges, such as the Funda Centre in SOWETO, provide adult basic education in a rich cultural environment, with an emphasis on music, art and sports. The educators are far more aware than is generally the case in England that basic skills and vocational preparation are of limited value, personally and for employment, unless they are provided in a context which nurtures creative potential to stimulate lifelong learning. Although leaders from the black communities in South Africa are interested in knowing about the scientific achievements of the West, they have no intention of allowing vocational man to destroy their cultural achievements, available for all to assess at the African Cultural Centre in Johannesburg.

The greatest need is, of course, resources but the case for partnerships with South African community colleges is that we have at least as much to learn about education from them as they from us. People working in Bilston and other similar urban areas in the UK do not need to travel to other countries to become aware of the cultural wealth of black people, especially in literature, art, music. Achievement in these does not mean, as is often argued, that Afro-Caribbean and Asian students are any less able to achieve in science and technology, as examinations results for the last twenty years confirm. But the cultural occasions organised at Bilston by these ethnic groups outnumber by a five to one ratio the cultural events initiated by the white population. Every week I receive dozens of invitations to address groups in the college and the community but only once in thirty years have I been asked to speak on English literature - by the (Asian) Progressive Writers Association.

Bilston's first major venture beyond Western Europe was the Montserrat project [1] in partnership with the University of Wolverhampton. The second (1993) was Moscow, at the request of an agency which wanted to establish a college for education and training in finance and banking. A partnership was formed including the Russian Department for Education, the Oil and Gas Corporation, a banker and Stowlawn Ltd (representing Bilston Community College). The British College of Banking and Finance (Moscow) was opened within 18 months, with businessmen funding the building, student fees supporting current expenditure (with an annual profit of 3million - *rubles*), and

Bilston's management and curriculum consultancy funded by Overseas Development Administration and European grants. The teaching is in English by 13 staff (12 Russian) and three successful years have been completed. To quote the *Daily Express* (March 14, 1996):

> As Britain's national debate continues over lacklustre standards in our schools, the lesson from the British College of Finance and Banking in Moscow is one that we cannot ignore.

> This impressive college is located on one of Moscow's main highways, close to Russia's most famous Statue of Lenin, founder of Communism, on October Square - built to deify the 1917 Revolution which abolished capitalism here for seven decades.

In England it is frequently asked *Is it profitable?*, the question meaning is there a surplus or deficit. On one of his (chief executive appraisal) tours of the college, the chair of the corporation was asked why money was being spent on a Russian project rather than on books for the library. In the early days, some members of the corporation questioned whether staff should be working in Moscow when there was so much to do in Bilston. A pensioner (a retired education officer) wrote to a local Member of Parliament asking how Bilston could be allowed to spend money abroad when old age pensioners were so badly off and, as stated in an earlier chapter, the FEFC was concerned that its money might be involved. These questions are recorded because they are common, and to some extent understandable, and must be addressed - not merely from a narrow financial perspective, but because educational issues are involved.

There have been colleges who have invested cash overseas and lost it. It may even be true that there are principals and managers who use every excuse to travel abroad because they prefer the climate elsewhere, or need a rest from FEFC circulars. Although there was no cash advance for the Moscow project, had it not succeeded there would have been an opportunity cost, perhaps £20,000 - £30,000, mainly staff time. In terms of income and expenditure, now well in excess of £2m, a small profit or loss can be shown depending on how the accounts are presented. If the project collapsed, always a possibility in countries experiencing political instability, it would be considered that the benefits far outweigh the disappointment.

The first conclusion from the experience is that projects should not be undertaken unless there is the prospect of long-term partnerships without significant financial loss. *Significant* is used deliberately because, as will be argued later, the educational benefits may be worth a manageable cash loss. In fact, a long-term project with a modest cash loss may be of greater benefit than a short-term project which makes a profit. In the case of the Moscow project, it is now three years old, with the prospect of substantial further development. The support of the business community continues, with the only frustration that the Russian government has been unable, for obvious reasons, to provide the resources it agreed to provide for expansion.

The second conclusion is that, from the outset, international projects should be integrated with college development as a whole. If this had been the case with the Moscow project, there would undoubtedly have been greater benefits to Bilston, including more income. The benefits to the curriculum in the finance, business and women's studies areas impacted at least a year later than should have been the case. Indeed, the team involved in women's studies in Moscow and Uzbekistan, (funded by Charity Know How grants) were discovered as being separate from the team concerned with women's studies at Bilston. There would have been greater financial benefits from integration and, equally important, quality would have been enhanced. Avoiding ad-hocery in the future is one of the reasons for the re-structuring to create the Bilston Consortium.

The third conclusion is that, given a policy of long-termism, the strategy should be to employ staff living in the country involved. This was applied to the day-to-day management of the Moscow College and is the main reason for its success. The experience of project management, and the training of the educators and managers involved, proved invaluable for the management and expansion of outreach partnerships on a large scale in England. Once a suitable model of organisation and management has been established, in this case based on training people living in the area and then delegating responsibility to them, distance loses most of its limitations. Before the Moscow experience, Bilston's management of outreach was an inefficient mix of central control and half-baked delegation, with an absence of clear and clearly understood systems.

If it were necessary to determine the cost benefit of the Moscow project it would be a return of at least 30 per cent. Apart from the specific benefits for management, curriculum, the professional development of managers and staff generally, there are the credibility and confidence factors, which increase the prospect of substantial resources for expansion and new projects. The credibility has resulted in grant approval for other projects - for example in Poland, Romania, and other countries in the Commonwealth of Independent States. The setting up and survival of the Moscow College, during the period which included the shooting at the White House, was a solid achievement, if not quite the miracle perceived by some. It is not an exaggeration to record that there is now a world-wide (at least third world-wide) demand for Bilston to set up colleges.

Partnership, based on the principle of equality of partners, is the key to the Bilston Consortium's strategy in England and internationally. Reliable partners abroad are essential but the scale of growth also depends on reliable partners in the West. The first major success, the Montserrat project, could not have occurred without the guidance and support of the University of Wolverhampton, which is also essential for expansion in Eastern Europe and for implementation of the embryonic plans for South Africa. Equally valuable is the involvement of Members of the European Parliament, the European Commission, and colleges in the USA. The positive internationalism of David Pierce and Jim Mahoney (American Association of Community Colleges), Dean VanTrease (chair of the American Council on International Intercultural Education), Paul Elsner (chancellor Maricopa Community College) and others too numerous to mention, has been a great encouragement to Bilston's international developments

For the longer-term, the opportunities to establish business and tourist support services, and for involvement (with other communities) in economic development and trade, are at least as valuable as the education and training projects. The Consortium's Business in Russia projects, in partnership with the private sector, made a small profit in 1995 and there is enormous potential for growth. The questions now asked at Bilston relate to how proposals support the overall strategy to integrate projects - locally, regionally, nationally, internationally. This strategy means that funding and financing is not considered on a narrow, short-term basis but as a matter of investment in the evolution of the Consortium as a whole.

A major benefit of the Moscow projects at home has been the greater positiveness of the private sector in seeking partnerships. Chadwell Securities Ltd, whose chair, Eric Partridge, survived a trip to Russia, is now the Business in Russia partner. The company has made property and facilities valued at more than £1.5 million available for management training and to establish an international business centre. An equally important benefit of this partnership is a clearer understanding of the needs and expectation of the private sector.

Individual members of the corporation, especially the chair and vice chair, have been fully involved in international projects since 1994, meeting visitors and travelling to their countries. The growing internationalisation has been debated regularly and in June 1995 the new, integrated (local, regional, national, international), strategy was explicitly adopted. There is wide recognition - corporation members, managers, staff - that work with partners overseas can improve quality overall and, providing it is well-managed, result in a more flexible and efficient use of resources. Equally important is that visitors are able to become involved with the Bilston community through the Springvale Club, which has consistently supported international co-operation. The only regret is that Bob Edwards, the inspiration for internationalism at Bilston, did not live to see Bilston become a global college.

Bilston's international projects have accelerated the strategy shift towards integrating education, training, economic re-generation. If communities such as Bilston and the black homelands in South Africa are ever to have full employment and prosperity it will be as a result of their own efforts, rather than from spontaneous investment from outside. Typical of the private sector is the Springvale opencast mining project 1989/91 - a quick profit and a few jobs for months rather than years. Forming partnerships across the world, democratically controlled by the people, can assist in stimulating the economic re-generation necessary to create permanent jobs. Since 1993, at least 50 additional jobs have been created as a result of Bilston's international activity and the number is planned to increase as the new strategy is implemented. The main purpose is to ensure that the grant aid available, from government and European sources, supports a co-ordinated plan for re-generation in the Black Country, reinforced by international enterprises with the same objectives.

Readers may be surprised at the absence of reference to new technology, the oft quoted facilitator of internationalism. Fax facilities played a crucial part in the success of Bilston's Russian projects, and the availability of the internet is being taken into account in planning. But heavy investment in new technology is the easiest way to lose money if it does not occur in the context of meticulous preparation. To achieve open access, equal opportunities objectives, with a priority of creating jobs, projects must be people driven and democratically controlled. The democratic control must extend to the new technology to ensure that it serves people and is kept firmly out of the driving seat.

Colleges based in the community, and accountable to the community, are the best means of determining that the priority is people's needs, not profit or technological advance as an end in itself. The evolution of the community college concept to focus on economic re-generation through education and training, in partnership with government and the private sector, is the theme of the last section of this chapter.

The United Kingdom and Western Europe

The 1992 European Communities Act determined much closer policy co-incidence with the rest of Europe, even through the UK government has adopted a negative attitude on measures related to education and training. Even when the opting out right is exercised, the influence of European Union policies is still increasing: one example is the Social Chapter where, despite the UK government's opt-out, employers are accepting clauses on workers' rights, including the right to representation on company boards. It makes no sense for multi-national companies to have different conditions from country to country when they wish to encourage worker mobility. For workers there have been some useful victories in the European Court, especially on pensions and equal pay.

One of the strongest influences will be the European Union's regional policy. Funding - for industry, local authorities, universities, colleges, community groups - is being increasingly channelled through the regions. The ad-hocery and confusion which currently exists will increase the pressure for the reform, or rather creation, of regional government in the UK. The change in the balance of power between the national government and the regions will have far-reaching political, as well as economic, significance: it will also assist the transformation from quangocracy to democracy in further education. The granting of funds to voluntary organisations gives them greater influence and bargaining power and enables them to form partnerships with local authorities, universities, colleges, employers. It also encourages college-employer partnerships, including projects for tackling unemployment. In the grants for training available from the European Commission, there has also been a marked shift to transnational projects, where approval requires at least one partner from another country - usually, but not always, a European Union country. If efficiently implemented, funds such as *LEONARDO* and *ADAPT* can bring together communities, often through the agency of colleges, to facilitate collaboration on generating economic activity. The anticipated European Parliament decision to extend partnerships to Central Europe and Southern Africa marks another step towards internationalisation.

Transnational projects create new opportunities for colleges. Apart from the obvious services - languages, translations, tourist information - they can open doors for the unemployed and provide contacts and support for small businesses. Given the reducing government resources for colleges in England, little Englanders are likely to be little colleges - if they continue to be colleges at all.

Colleges working with their communities cannot avoid involvement in the operation of regional funds. In addition to European funding, the Single Regeneration Budget and other government funds are channelled through the regional offices. The Association for Colleges' ability to strengthen and develop its regional structures depends on all colleges becoming active members. Colleges involved with their communities can provide a lead in forming partnerships with voluntary organisations, local authorities, employers and other interest groups at regional level. Support for democratic processes in local communities must be regarded as part of the campaign to restore democracy to further education.

The negative stance of UK governments on Europe has made it difficult for regions and colleges to take full advantage of European funding to support further education, training, economic re-generation. The take up of *ADAPT* funds available in 1996, for example, was £12million from an available £58million. Because the chief sufferers are the unemployed and small businesses and, therefore, local economies, it is essential to pressurise the UK government to a more positive position.

The European Parliament, through the European Commission, is placing an increasing emphasis on democracy when awarding grants, both within the European Union and outside. Its policy of *subsidiarity*, devolving decision-making to regions and communities, is contrary to the UK government's and FEFC's policy of concentrating decision-making at the centre. The FEFC would, no doubt, contend that it operates more efficiently, a position which appears to gather support from the delays and confusion which sometimes surround the distribution of European funds. But, as the examples in Chapters Four and Five demonstrate, the FEFC's *efficiency* in terms of the use of funds

is more apparent than real, even on a narrow definition of the term. More
seriously, if, as argued in this book and supported by the evidence quoted, the
implementation of vocationalism is failing people and the economy the whole
system is inefficient on a gigantic scale.

Community colleges and economic re-generation

There are international organisations which encourage co-operation amongst
colleges across the world and other organisations which foster economic co-
operation and development amongst nations. Although there are some links
between the education and the economic pressure groups, they are not often
involved together in addressing the overall requirements of communities. But
the necessary investment in human resources can be justified and acquired only
if plans for education and training are integrated with plans for community and
economic re-generation and development. Proposals must demonstrate that
there will be a satisfactory rate of return, in financial as well as educational
terms.

In areas of high unemployment in the West, and the more numerous areas of
high unemployment in developing countries, investment in education and
training is needed on a massive scale. This will become available only if
education, training, economic re-generation and development are planned as
three elements of an integrated whole. It is in this context that the Bilston
Consortium, in association with the Community Colleges Association of South
Africa, is taking steps to establish an organisation to bring together, with a
common focus, representatives of national governments, regional (provincial)
and local governments, the private sector and voluntary organisations. There
is growing support in the USA, especially amongst the members of the
Association for International, Intercultural Education.

The purpose of the International Association for Education, Training and Work
(IAETW) is to create direct links amongst communities throughout the world,
and to encourage governments and multi-national organisations (e.g.
employers, trade unions and the European Union) to support education,
training and economic re-generation through community enhancement. The
new Association's aims are to:

(i)   create direct links amongst people living in communities
        throughout the world;

(ii)   obtain support for economic development through community enhancement from governments, multi-national organisations, industry and commerce;

(iii)   provide a forum to promote policies which integrate education, training and economic development, with the emphasis on small enterprises (including self-employment) in communities across the world;

(iv)   establish an international curriculum centre, prioritising further education and training to support economic development;

(v)   build a team of consultants to advise on the development of further education and training systems (based on community colleges) as integrated elements of projects for economic regeneration;

(vi)   foster links between the public and private sectors, especially to generate resources for education, training and economic regeneration;

(vii)   foster international links through cultural activities, especially in the sphere of sport and leisure;

(viii)   act as an agency to organise conference and seminars.

The USA community colleges have proved one of the most successful educational initiatives in history, creating opportunities for millions of citizens. Their commitment to democracy includes promoting it internationally, especially through the American Association of Community Colleges and the Association for International, Intercultural Education. Progressive USA colleges, in partnership with a small number in other developed countries (e.g. England, Canada, Japan), are establishing partnerships with colleges in less developed countries, especially South Africa. Because these countries require resources for education and training on a massive scale, community colleges are the best available solution, but the USA and UK models cannot be transplanted without radical development of the community college concept.

The need for radical change to address the challenges in poor communities in the USA is accepted by the USA government. In an address to the American Association of Community Colleges in April 1996, Labour Secretary Robert Reich announced plans for a new partnership with community colleges to place them *squarely in the centre of workforce development effort in the age of technology*. He recognised that *community colleges stand at the great fault line, the great divide between the haves and the have nots*. The fact that the challenges in poor countries differ only in scale is the reason for an international strategy.

There are two fundamental questions facing community colleges:

(i)   How should established community colleges in the West (for instance in USA and England) develop to meet the needs of their own communities?

(ii)   What can they contribute to the provision of education and training for people throughout the world, especially in countries (for instance South Africa) where the vast majority have been denied access in the past?

The community colleges involved internationally with long-term partnership objectives are likely to be the more progressive in their own countries. Even in the USA, where the community college movement is strongest, there are areas where whole communities are denied education, training, jobs. In England, where community colleges are a minority, there are areas where a third of school-leavers participate in no further education and training; where more than half the adult population have no recognised qualifications; where over 25 per cent of adults do not have the basic literacy and numeracy skills required to undertake training leading to recognised vocational qualifications. There are a number of reasons for the absence of opportunities but, as argued in earlier chapters, the barrier which must be addressed by colleges is the inadequate curriculum for working-class people, including ethnic minorities.

As demonstrated in Chapter Three, community education, as distinct from academic or vocational curriculum, is essential to develop human resources where people have been denied access. The starting point in any country is not the curriculum which exists in established institutions but the experiences of people in their communities. The structure of the Bilston Consortium (Chapter

Five) illustrates the implications for organisation and management. Traditional colleges can grow and change only very slowly and require large-scale capital investment, for instance in computerised learning centres. Their centralised financial and administration systems clog up when there is a sudden increase in demand and they perceive curriculum change as a modification of what exists, rather than a matter of starting with the experiences of people and building from them.

Education through partnerships, which means pooling resources, can work only when common objectives are identified. A college may focus on education and training but a community partner is likely to have other priorities: paying the rent, facilities for the disabled, investment in new buildings - to name only a few. The first stage of a partnership may involve no more than a joint application for a grant, which may have no resources for education and training. A full partnership will evolve only if the college recognises that a grant for education and training in an area of high unemployment is of limited value without longer-term plans to create jobs through generating commercial and industrial activity.

If they are prepared to accept a wider responsibility, along the lines proposed by Robert Reich, community colleges have a key role to play across the world. If they are able to form partnerships in their own communities, they will be able to link communities to generate resources through trade, as well as to enhance education and training. The emphasis is on direct links amongst small enterprises, operating in groups for purposes such as product development, marketing. A primary objective must be to use democratically controlled new technology to *create* jobs, the alternative to control by large organisations which results in job losses.

Education, training and successful economic activity all require the ability to respond to rapid change. Frequent re-training for quick switches to the manufacture of new products is the only means of avoiding bankruptcy and unemployment in a rapidly changing world. A strategy of diversification provides the greatest security, with progress depending on convincing investors that small enterprises (including the self-employed), operating in groups, can make a major contribution to the 21st century economy. It is because they are in touch with the needs of people living in their localities that community colleges can provide education and training to initiate economic activity.

Community colleges in the West will make a major contribution to the community colleges' movement across the world, providing they extend and deepen involvement with their own localities. The strategic re-assessment advocated by Reich for USA colleges to serve their own country must be made with the recognition that, despite the vast differences of wealth amongst nations, there are poor communities requiring economic re-generation in the West as well as in the Third World. The priority for the International Association for Education, Training and Work (IAETW) is to promote a broader concept of the community college role, and to encourage those concerned with economic re-generation, including governments and multi-national organisations, to form partnerships with community colleges.

---

[1] In partnership with the University of Wolverhampton, Bilston Community College staff and students, sponsored by the local construction industry helped to rebuild the schools on the hurricane-devastated island of Montserrat.

Chapter Seven

Education, training and the economy

Economic policy and employment

UK government policy since 1979 has been to vocationalise all further education and increase vocational influence on the secondary school curriculum. The emphasis on preparation for work at the expense of all else has coincided with the decline of manufacturing, with disappearance of millions of unskilled jobs. The stabilisation of unemployment in the two to three million (10 per cent) range is as much the result of different presentation of statistics as of the creation of jobs; and it conceals the fact that a growing proportion of new jobs, especially for women, are part-time and temporary. The lack of opportunities for people over 50, many of whom are unceremoniously cast aside after 20 - 30 years of dedicated service, is only marginally less offensive than the number of under 25s who have never had the chance to work at all.

Neither the Tory nor Labour parties have policies which give priority to full employment. This would require tackling structural problems in the economy, radical and imaginative measures to create jobs; a shorter working week and year; more flexible conditions of employment. Market forces now, inevitably, operating in a global economy, mean that large-scale redundancies occur in a most unpredictable and arbitrary fashion. One solution is to control market forces and establish a planned economy: the other, to provide support, especially education and training linked to economic re-generation, for redundant workers. A planned economy is not on the agenda and proposals, by both government and Opposition, to tackle unemployment are short-term measures rather than education and training in the context of major job creation programmes.

As implied in earlier chapters, the policy path has been determined by the 1992 European Communities Act. This was supported by the Tories as the best means of protecting private enterprise in a volatile world economy, where the long-established industrial nations are threatened by the industrial muscle of the Pacific rim. But the problem for Tory free-marketeers is that the European

Union is intent on intervening in the market - for example to steer resources to combat social exclusion at home and to assist economic re-generation in the world outside, especially in Central and Eastern Europe and Africa. Although, in the longer term, both policies may prove to be the best means of protecting capitalism, it is not the habit of the right in the UK to look beyond short-term gains. The dilemma of the Tories, demonstrated by their rejection of the Social Chapter, is that they want a cartel to protect free enterprise without Europe's social policies. Membership of the European Union, accompanied by a negative position on its social policies, means that the UK pays its subscription but its people receive only half the benefits.

Rejection of traditional socialist solutions, including a planned economy, determines that the Labour Party has no alternative to positive Europeanism. Its *New Deal for a Lost Generation* (1996) is in accord with Europe's *Teaching and Learning : Towards the Learning Society* in recognising the serious consequences of excluding so many people from the technological society. Its weakness is that proposals for the unemployed are short-term measures financed by a windfall tax, not a coherent policy to create jobs on anything like the scale required. The measures proposed by *New Deal for a Lost Generation* will achieve no more than the schemes of the late, unlamented, Department of Employment unless the structural changes in the economy are recognised and addressed.

Since 1979, the national strategy has been to intensify competition through market forces to reduce costs. Companies forced into bankruptcy through want of a short-term loan or subsidy have had a major impact on the unemployment figures. It is beyond question that, in a substantial number of cases, the cost of financial support would have been less than the cost of lost production plus the benefits paid to people who lost their jobs. The *substantial number* requires quantification to establish (i) the kind of support needed by, mainly small, companies, and (ii) the point beyond which it is not economic to provide support. The argument is not that all ailing companies should be supported but that decisions about support should be based on economic and social criteria, not a blind free-marketeer ideology. If employment levels of the 1960s are ever to be achieved again, self-employment and small enterprises, especially community enterprises, must play an important part.

The path towards an economic policy to create jobs, for reasons of ideology more open to a Labour than a Tory government, is through collaboration with Europe in the context of positive internationalism. Throughout the 1980s and early 1990s there was no effective co-ordination of European and UK government measures to re-generate the economy. Given the growing commitment to regionalism of the European Parliament, this is primarily a regional matter and requires government to have a coherent regional strategy. The short-term decisions necessary to co-ordinate the existing unelected bodies responsible for allocating funds should be taken in the context of plans for democratic regional government. For the reasons given in Chapter Six, plans for economic re-generation should be integrated with plans for the education and training of school leavers, unemployed adults, and people in work who require skills updating and qualifications.

The policies arising from the free market competition ideology have, as intended, increased unemployment - by compelling large firms to shed labour and by allowing thousands of small firms and the self-employed to go bankrupt. Some large firms go to the wall with their business going to foreign competitors, often operating in other countries: others receive government contracts and, depending on their influence with ministers, hidden subsidies. In many cases, monopoly and cartel arrangements mean that competition is more apparent than real. Nevertheless, the chief characteristics of take over and merger are redundancy for workers and managers but obscenely large pay-offs for bosses.

The most damaging effect of the free market economy ideology has been on public services, both in increasing unemployment and on the quality of the services. The hot, summer days of 1995 demonstrated that privatised water companies regard service to customers as less important than fat salaries for directors and executives, while prizes can safely be offered to any regular user of the health service who has experienced real improvement since competition was introduced. If local government is more efficient, it is in terms of a narrow, value for money, assessment, which measures the effect on balance sheets rather than on people. Is the increased number of people needed to service unelected quangos, and to deal with the unemployed (including spying on them), evidence of a more efficiently run economy?

None of this is to suggest that the public utilities, the health service, local government, further education were providing satisfactory services before the attack on them in the 1980s. The contracts of health service consultants, local government officers, further education lecturers did not evolve merely, or even mainly, as responses to customer need. Some local authority education departments, to take just one example, were shrouded in bureaucracy to a degree which left them largely unaffected by changes in political control. Reforms were needed for greater co-ordination, to improve quality of service, and to ensure more effective democratic accountability. But the consequence of privatisation and competition is service related to ability to pay, not a general improvement. In all the reforms, the lowest priority has been concern for social responsibility and democratic accountability.

The alternative to the plethora of quangos, and it is not self-evident that the Labour Party has fully grasped this, is empowerment of people in their communities and the democratisation of institutions. In terms of economic policy the priority is to create jobs through integrated education, training, economic and social re-generation projects. Given the European criteria already described, the agencies must be democratically-elected regional authorities operating in partnership with community groups. The fact that the process for dealing with European funding in the regions is perceived as a bureaucratic maze is partly the consequence of the UK government's negative attitudes to Brussels.

Although tinkering with quangos, as Labour proposes, is the only short-term option to increase community participation, the major problems of the inner cities will not be solved by tinkering. The, admittedly weak, economic upturns of the 1980s and early 1990s brought no lasting benefit to most areas of high, and long term, unemployment. The economy as a whole could grow twice as fast as the current 2 per cent per year and still leave millions of people, teenagers and adults, unemployed, poor, and lacking the skills and qualifications necessary to find work. Most jobs in manufacturing historically available to the unqualified have gone for ever. Further education and training for all is now generally accepted as necessary but, unless it is integrated with economic policies to create jobs, the outcome will be no more than a better qualified army of unemployed people.

To achieve full employment policies must address the following issues:

-   a shorter working week and year and more flexible working conditions;

-   investment in communities, with the recognition that a rational policy for jobs will mean more leisure for all;

-        support for community industry;

-        the linking of communities nationally and internationally;

-        the identification of skills and know-how to increase productivity and exports;

-        opportunities for lifelong education and training.

Because they have a history of serving their localities, colleges are the key to community, social, economic re-generation, especially in areas of industrial decline and high unemployment. They must, however, be transformed to community colleges and made democratically accountable. Transformation depends on partnerships, with local and regional government and the private sector.   But the most important partnerships are with community based organisations - places of worship, sports clubs, trade unions - where working-class adults meet. Community experience is the basis for a curriculum to create access to education, training and employment.

The reform of post-16 education

The 1992 Further and Higher Education Act made colleges independent corporations, with a brief to provide vocational training for employers. The government's vision was of a re-invented Manpower Services Commission, the Further Education Funding Council, acquiring the resources of colleges to meet national education and training targets. The emphasis was on the narrow, competency-based, approach to learning controlled by another quango, the National Council for Vocational Qualifications. The utilitarian philosophy was demonstrated to be alive, and as ill-conceived as ever, in the Department for Education and Employment response to the European Year of Lifelong Learning in 1996.

The vocational role assigned to colleges perpetuates a bilateral system at 16 plus, with academic GCE A levels (the route to traditional universities) in colleges and school sixth forms, and vocational courses in colleges.   The Dearing Report, *Review of Qualifications for 16 - 19 year olds*, failed to grasp the nettle, recommending that the two systems should continue within a co-ordinating framework.   The Labour Party position is essentially an endorsement of Dearing, with a trifle more emphasis on the singleness of the framework, and a slightly higher priority for integrating the two systems within it. The weakness of both positions, as of most other publications on post-16 curriculum 1990/96, stems from their imprisonment in a 16-18 schools' perspective. The contribution, past and potential, of colleges is assumed to be largely confined to young people disadvantaged by a raw deal at school.

The absence of a common system for accreditation is a reflection of the refusal to tackle the structural problems of education and training at 16 plus. Apart from perpetuating curriculum and social divisions, school sixth forms have high unit costs, partly concealed by subsidies from funding allocated to the 11 - 16 age group. The choice available is limited when the total number staying on is fewer than 100, the maximum in one year for most schools. Small GCE A level classes often become smaller when vocational options are introduced and students recognise them as more relevant. Timetables integrated with further education to open doors to vocational options are the exception.

Despite the abolition of the Department of Employment in 1995, and the transfer of its functions to the Department for Education and Employment, training and enterprise councils (TECs) continued with their responsibilities for training. Some TECs purchase most of their training from private training providers, where trainees have a limited choice. Even more serious, private providers are limited in expertise and facilities for basic skills support, the greatest need of unemployed working-class people. The claim that TECs provide training at lower cost than colleges ignores quality factors such as student facilities, restriction of choice, limited opportunities for progression. The focus is entirely on obtaining qualifications, with a failure to recognise that quality of the experience is as valuable for 21st century job performance as for the personal development of the individual.

Despite accumulating evidence that vocationalism is the wrong approach for the 21st century, the government blundered on. The Dearing Report pronounced the youth training scheme, run by the TECs, a failure. The greater the emphasis on competitiveness the less competitive the UK became internationally. The 1996 *World Competitiveness Yearbook*, published by the International Institute for Management Development, revealed that Britain had fallen from 15th to 19th in the World League. Although a four place fall in one year may not be a disaster, the steady decline from 11th in 1989 cannot be ignored. The Institute's conclusion that the key weakness is a failure to invest in training and re-training echoes other reports. On investment in people, the UK came 27th out of 46 countries, a fall from 18th in 1989.

The debate on college, sixth form, TEC costs can divert attention from the fact that most expensive of all are the universities, especially the long established institutions - confirmation, if needed, that elitism persists. Although figures from the different sectors lack common assumptions, the relative costs of a full-time student equivalent is approximately a ratio of 7 (university) to 3 (school sixth form) to 2.5 (further education college). The inequality of treatment is partly accounted for by mandatory tuition fee and maintenance grants for students in higher education, and partly by higher staff costs, particularly for research. The conventional wisdom that research is necessary for quality of teaching is a claim not easily supported by evidence.

Higher education numbers grew rapidly in the early 1990s, especially in the new universities (previously polytechnics), and the target of 30 per cent of the age group acquiring degrees was reached earlier than expected. To match international competitors it was recognised, for example by the Confederation of British Industries, that a new target of 60 per cent was required. Yet the government, at a loss as to how continuing expansion could be funded, imposed a funding halt in 1996 - at the precise time the expansion of further education was increasing pressure on university places. This stop/go approach is inevitable while the policy is elitist, meritocratic rationing rather than equal opportunities for all. The timing of the restriction on university expansion demonstrates either a complete lack of policy co-ordination, or that the purpose of further education is to create cannon fodder for employers - or both.

Labour was equally reluctant to address the question of funding higher education: indeed, Jeff Rooker was sacked as a front bench spokesperson when he wrote a discussion paper on the subject in 1995. Both government and Opposition were pleased to kick the issue into touch (until after the General Election) by supporting a new Dearing Committee to report in 1997. The composition of the committee - there was, for example, no representative from further education - confirmed that the exercise was to prevent political embarrassment rather than address the factors affecting the future of higher education. The government's education trouble-shooter in chief, Sir Ron Dearing, having rescued ministers from disaster on the national curriculum, and papered over the cracks and divisions 16-19, was leap-frogged over colleges to deal with higher education.

Yet the crucial factor is the millions excluded from the system as described in Chapter Four. As already argued, bringing them in is partly a question of resources, but equally a matter of transforming curriculum and reforming institutions. Many adults, usually ignored if they are not in higher education, require basic skills support to acquire the qualifications necessary for the 21st century. For this reason alone, resourcing further education is at least as urgent a matter as the brief of Sir Ron Dearing. Governments will not begin to resolve the problems until it is recognised that post-16 education and training must be considered as a whole, and in the context of overall economic and social policy. There will be no relevant answers while the wrong questions are asked, as of the Dearing Committee, or, as in the case of further education, no questions are asked at all.

It is vested interests (in schools, universities, education departments, the civil service) intent on preserving an elitist system, and the government's blind faith in employer-shaped vocationalism, which deny opportunities to hundreds of thousands of adults. A system of community colleges for over 16s, pooling the resources of sixth forms, colleges, TECs, adult education services, training agencies, could increase participation by at least a million without additional resources. To achieve the level of participation needed requires a community-education-based approach to curriculum and more efficient use of buildings and equipment - over 7 days a week for 50 weeks a year.

Action is urgent and, in the short-term, partnerships of colleges with community organisations and employers are the chief means of acquiring additional resources. This applies to the use of buildings, equipment, expertise belonging to the partners, but also to the opportunities for additional income by, for example, joint applications for European and other funding, and joint ventures for commercially profitable projects. Initiatives should include international projects, linking communities across the world to promote trade and create jobs, especially through self-employment and small enterprises. Because the countries of Eastern and Central Europe and Africa, for example, are in even greater need of generating resources and employment, they are willing partners for income-generating projects. The government's recognition in its *Competitiveness* white papers that the economy of the future will be a global one has had no discernible impact on its policies for education and training.

The debate on resources can disguise the fact that the overall objective is to release the enormous potential of untapped human resources. Apart from the damage to individuals, leaving millions of people to languish unemployed and unqualified is the road to defeat from a social and economic own goal. The policy of educating and training people on the assumption that the market will provide jobs cannot succeed. Large companies will continue to downsize their workforces and employ, on a permanent basis, only highly trained specialists, usually in new technology. The state intervention required is not large-scale investment in a few projects but support for individuals and small enterprises - loans, training in self-organisation and management, assistance with the marketing of products. Structural investment is needed to improve the environment and to extend and enhance leisure facilities: this requires partnerships of voluntary community groups with elected local and regional authorities, the private sector, colleges, universities.

College corporations must not be left as self-perpetuating oligarchies. Legislation is necessary to guarantee democratic representation, along the lines of governing body constitutions before the 1988 Education Reform Act: one third elected representatives (from local or regional government) and one third from the college, including elected staff and student representatives. The final third should be either representatives of the college's employer, trade union and community partners in accord with democratic constitutional arrangements, or by direct election from the electoral wards in the college vicinity. Direct election, although more difficult and expensive to organise, is preferable because (i) it enables the community to exert influence, and (ii) it raises the profile of colleges.

Given democratically-determined membership, the powers of corporations are not unreasonable, although there needs to be clarification of their responsibility for strategy. The major changes required are (i) to restore to academic boards the powers on curriculum they enjoyed before 1988, with elected staff and student representatives, and (ii) to ensure that students' unions have an appropriate degree of independence on student affairs. These steps would limit the powers of chief executives, who should be specifically accountable to the democratically-determined governing bodies. Making managers accountable is a matter of defining the management context more precisely, not creating the opportunity for day-to-day interference, which would result in the kind of chaos which occurred when education officers were able to interfere.

Corporations operate in a vacuum, subject to the whims of the Further Education Funding Council, training and enterprise councils and the business community. They have a responsibility for strategy but lack the powers to exercise it, largely because they have insignificant influence over funding. The FEFC's systems, applied blindly country-wide, are incapable of taking into account local, or even regional, circumstances. TECs have a responsibility to approve corporations' strategies but insufficient powers and information to exercise it. The absence of a single body with powers to co-ordinate education and training was savagely criticised by a report published in 1996 by the government's own advisers, the National Advisory Council for Education and Training Targets (NACETT, 1996).

Transferring some of the powers of the FEFC to the regions, as proposed, for example, by the Labour Party, would be a positive interim measure - given sufficient co-ordination with regional government offices. The democratic solution, however, depends on elected regional authorities with strategic responsibility for all post 16 education and training. This must include universities and requires a regional education and training board which, albeit with limited powers, could be created in advance of the elected regional authorities. Representation on the same principle as governing bodies would be a step towards regional relevance - one third from colleges and universities; one third from business and the community; one third appointed by the Department for Education and Employment.

Although some of these changes could be implemented quickly, their effect would be limited without a new legislative framework. The principles for a new further and higher education Act are to:

- create a unified system at 16 plus to co-ordinate the work of sixth forms, TECs, colleges, universities, adult education services;

- fund a curriculum which recognises that the lifelong approach to learning is the best preparation for training for employment;

- create democratically elected regional authorities;

- establish a national strategy board to provide a planning context for regional boards - on the basis of recognition that education and training must be integrated with social and economic re-generation and development;

- ensure appropriate democratic accountability at all levels, including governing bodies of colleges and universities.

A democratically accountable system of community colleges and universities, serving the whole population over 16, assumes a policy emphasis directly opposite to that which determined the existing quangocracy. It must start with the involvement of people in education in their communities and create a framework which guarantees that institutions are accountable to the people they serve. The new policy must be based on the principle of devolution and separation of powers, the only basis for equal partnerships. The process of change should place the emphasis on partnerships, not on the take-over of one group of institutions by another.

Resourcing a comprehensive system

By 1996 it was accepted that, without emergency measures, the UK would not meet its modest (by international standards) national education and training targets by the millennium. Reports on the economy and its competitiveness range from discouraging to disastrous in the sphere of education and training, with low participation rates for teenagers and adults as compared with other western nations and some on the Pacific rim. Even at 16, where staying on rates had shown a marked improvement in the late 1980s and early 1990s, there was a falling back. Starting from a lower base, the staying-on full-time rate beyond 17 was increasing more slowly than in most other European countries and the relative position on adult training remained a matter for concern.

The absence of maintenance grants excludes many unqualified and unemployed people. Although, in terms of overall priorities, there is a case for loans for over 18s in higher education, this does not apply at the 16 - 18 stage. The availability of mandatory grants for people with two GCE A levels or the equivalent, with only meagre, hardship, grants for a few 16 - 18s, has always restricted access to more advanced levels. The message to teenagers unable to afford to stay on beyond 16 is that they can have a grant if they acquire the equivalent of two GCE A levels but that there is no adequate financial support to assist them to the level where they qualify for mandatory grants.

The Dearing Report's confirmation that youth training schemes have failed demonstrates the necessity for urgent measures. The Labour Party's response, is to use the £550 million youth training budget to introduce *Target 2000* for all 16 - 17 year olds, whether unemployed or in work. Although employers will be *expected* to grant day release, experience indicates that this will not occur without legislation and there is no commitment to legislate. The weakness of all proposals on the table is that they do not address the central issue - the fact that those who can afford it will continue in full-time education, while the rest will be on some kind of vocational training scheme.

The Labour Party's proposal for a Personal Development and Guidance Service (to replace the existing Careers Services) is well-meaning and, no doubt, intended to provide advice for individuals who wish to continue to higher education. But the context of the proposal remains meritocratic, a rationing of growth rather than a policy of education and training for all. The rationing is determined by limiting resources to the £550m per year currently spent on youth training. Even if employers contributed, which they would not, on an equal basis, without legislation, the divided system would remain, with full-timers on academic courses resourced at one level and those on vocational courses at another.

A comprehensive, equal opportunities, system can be achieved only by making a unified community college service responsible for the education and training of all 16 - 18 year olds. The curriculum changes already described would remove the distinction between academic and vocational and between full-time and part-time study. All programmes would include placements, for example for language students a more substantial period than currently in the country of the language studied, and for social studies students a period with statutory or voluntary social services agencies. Students wishing to take jobs would have their employment restricted to 3½ days (28 hours) per week, with colleges rather than employers responsible for their programmes of study.

It is estimated that the revenue cost would be at least four times the current expenditure on youth training - over £2 billion. The additional resources could be acquired partly by contributions from employers, although grants would be necessary for the large number not in employment. Given a unified system, integrating the resources of colleges, sixth forms, training and enterprises councils, there would be sufficient space, although investment to improve buildings and update equipment would be necessary. But integrating the planning of education, training, economic re-generation regionally would result in contributions from, for example, European structural and social funds and the Single Regeneration Budget.

Half of the additional revenue funding could be acquired from more effective co-ordination and management of existing resources and modest contributions from employers. This means that comprehensive provision for 16 - 18 year olds could be achieved with additional public expenditure of around £1 billion. The relevant question is not whether this can be afforded but a question of priorities in terms of public expenditure. No government expects the economy to grow by less than 2 per cent per year, which means that an additional £50 billion will become available by the millennium. Given the UK plight on 16 - 18 education and training, and the almost unanimous recognition that action must be taken, it is obvious that the additional £1 billion per year must be found from government income.

Because there will be a higher priority for open learning supported by new technology, substantial capital expenditure will be inevitable. It is here, rather than in the student support, revenue sphere, that employers, in their own interests, should be expected to contribute. The most appropriate model is college/employer partnerships, with government support to the partnerships rather than to the partners separately. This approach is also consistent with the integration of education, training and economic re-generation, the key to ensuring that people who acquire qualifications are able to find employment.

A unified system is a pre-condition for a coherent curriculum framework which permits student progression, as well as to ensure the most effective use of resources. If stage one is integrating education and training 16 - 18, stage two is integrating further with higher education. Simultaneously, it is necessary to address the divisions in higher education, especially between the old (research-oriented) and the new (more learning, community-oriented) universities. Even if there is a link between research and the quality of teaching and, as already stated, this is not proven, this is no argument for confining it to a limited number of institutions.

As with the 16 - 18 stage, integrating further education colleges and universities will release sufficient resources for major expansion. The industrial partnership model, with government support to the partnerships, is the most appropriate channel for capital investment. Also applicable is the assumption that the distinction between full-time and part-time study will disappear, with all students not in work having substantial placement experience.

It is not necessary to accept in principle that grants for all are not possible to recognise that it is likely to be a political fact that they will not be provided. Under the current system there is an indefensible inequality of support between further and higher education students. Whatever the level of grant or loan, it is not a matter of whether one or other can be afforded but the way in which public finances and taxation policies are formulated. An equitable system must be either a grants systems, or a mixture of grants and loans designed to ensure that the poor are not disadvantaged. Loans for 16 - 18 year olds must be strongly resisted, and any loans systems for higher education must be geared to the ability to repay.

Expansion in the short-term depends on more efficient use of facilities: a seven- day must replace a four-day week, and fifty rather than thirty weeks per year become the norm. Providing this is managed without linking opening times to the hours people are expected to work, resistance to the change will be greatly reduced. In any case, the learning culture gives priority to students learning rather than lecturers teaching. Access for many students depends on facilities, with appropriate learning support, being *open all hours*. The key factor is the management of the facilities of schools, colleges, universities as one sector rather than three.

One of the surprises when education and training are taken into the community and to employers' premises is the range, and in some cases quality, of the facilities available. There is more to be gained from contracting with organisations to use their facilities than from attempting to persuade them to make cash contributions to colleges. Another surprise in partnerships is the range of expertise available, sometimes the solution to colleges' and universities' staff shortages. Taking advantage of partners' resources is the only means of rapid expansion in the short-term; while pooling resources is likely to prove the path to long-term growth.

Computer networks and related advances in technology remove some of the limitations of multi-site provision. As local, regional, national, international links become easier day by day, the prospects improve for the millions across the world denied education and training. Partnerships amongst colleges and universities in different countries are becoming as easy as local school, college, university partnerships - in some cases easier, owing to the absence of historical rivalry.   Although in any context formidable, the problem of resources may prove more capable of solution with an international perspective.

The key question for governments is whether they have the courage to reject elitism and meritocracy.   A comprehensive system implies funding community colleges and traditional institutions on an equal basis, along with acceptance that policies and strategy must be determined democratically.   The last chapter will examine the implications for colleges of a commitment to the democratic process.

Chapter Eight

Further education and democracy

Democracy and internationalism: South Africa

It may appear that not much of this book is about democracy: it is, in fact, all about democracy - too often the lack of it. Frank Reeves, in *The Modernity of Further Education*, described how it was being killed off: his book could have been entitled, *the death of democracy in further education*. *Further Education and Democracy* is written with the intention of igniting the embers. It is inspired locally by the unshaken commitment to the democratic cause of members of Bilston Community College Corporation (especially the chair and vice chair, Alan Millington and Dennis Turner), and internationally by the achievement of the African National Congress (ANC) in overcoming apartheid. The people who created democratic South Africa are now striving to build a comprehensive community college system to provide education and training for all. Their success or failure will have far-reaching implications for democracy in the whole of Africa and the Third World.

The elitism of universities in South Africa, together with the narrow vocationalism of most of the technical colleges, means that an English visitor feels very much (too much) at home. The battle to control post-16 education is currently being waged, with the key question whether resources should be made available through traditional higher education institutions, or allocated directly to democratically controlled community colleges. In an attempt to answer this question, in 1995 a commission was appointed for higher education, with community colleges largely ignored - as in England when the Dearing Committee was set up in 1996. It is because the struggle for a democratic system is so similar to the battle in the UK that it is easy to find common cause with South African community colleges It was in this context that the Bilston Consortium signed an agreement with the Community Colleges Association of South Africa (CCASA) in 1995.

The agreement was signed following extensive discussions with Silas Zuma, Director of the National Institute of Community Education (NICE). Silas is a key figure in influencing the South African government to adopt a community college system. Before reaching agreement with Bilston, members of CCASA Executive - Motsumi Makhene, Dikeledi Molatoli, Martin Mulcahy - visited colleges in the USA and England. The agreement with Bilston is complemented by an agreement with similar objectives between CCASA and the American Association of Community Colleges (AACC).

If the South African government decides to allow traditional higher education institutions to retain control, with community colleges the poor relations as in the UK, the outcome will be an elitist system, with education and training rationed to a percentage of the population. If, however, it decides to recognise a national system of community colleges, with equality in terms of status and funding, the outcome will be, in accord with the policies of CCASA: education and training integrated with social and economic re-generation for all citizens. The first option could result in a quangocracy as in the UK: the second a democratic system in accord with the policies and principles of the ANC. The outcome will be influential not only for developing countries about to establish systems for mass education, but also for the struggle to transform to democratically-based systems in the UK and the West in general.

The best hope for college democracy is to internationalise the campaign. This is recognised by USA community college progressives working in AACC and its international partner, the American Council on International Intercultural Education (ACIIE) and by a growing number of colleges in the UK. Although the proportion of the population denied access is higher in countries like South Africa, the numbers in the USA are high enough to be taken seriously, and the scale of exclusion in Europe has already been described. The way forward is not by imposition of the USA or UK system in developing countries but by partnerships to address the organisational, management, curriculum challenges collectively. Western nations may have more money but South Africa, in the ANC, has more democracy and a stronger commitment to the democratic process.

Democracy and community colleges

In South Africa, the task is to apply the principles and processes evolved during the struggle against apartheid to the organisation and management of community colleges. In the UK, the challenge is to transform the self-perpetuating oligarchies of quangocracy to elected bodies accountable to the community. In these, and all other cases, the focus must be on the principles of openness, separation of powers, and freedom of information and expression. The principles and practice of democracy in colleges have been analysed by Professor Eric Robinson (1990), almost a lone voice advocating the democratisation of universities and colleges during the past decade:

> Such has been this complacency that little new thought has been given to the topic and little credence has been given to such writers as Chomsky who have suggested that all is not well with western democracy.

As an alternative to the autocratic further education system in the UK, Robinson advocates *a democracy that provides for continuing participation at many levels, guaranteed by firm separation of powers.* This is a perspective very different from those who advocate democracy in education by creating single, all powerful, elected bodies - for example, governing bodies, or academic boards, or senates. The distance from democracy in the UK is demonstrated by the fact that further education is controlled by the FEFC, an unelected body, and there is no means of challenging its decisions by any body related in any way to a democratic process. Indeed, as illustrated in Chapter Two, there is no means of challenging the FEFC other than in the courts. Taken a stage further, because would-be challengers cannot afford to risk the costs of court action, the FEFC is virtually unchallengeable. Because there is no effective distribution of powers - in reality, the FEFC controls everything because it controls the funding - the characteristics of the further education system are those of regimes commonly regarded as the antithesis of democracy : at worst Stalinism, at best Titoism.

The situation in English further education confirms the necessity for separation of powers, what Robinson describes as *democratic subsidiarity.* He draws a parallel between subsidiarity and management delegation where the aim is to avoid detailed decision-making by remote high authority:

> This is related to control by excessive bureaucracy in which day-to-day low level decision-making is carried out by petty bureaucrats ostensibly interpreting the rule book and effectively exercising power without responsibility. A common symptom of this is the employee who makes no attempt to justify a decision to a client or subordinate employee beyond explaining that it derives from regulations or *policy* of the council or the company.

Those who reject democracy usually argue that it is inefficient and delays decision-making. To avoid inefficiency, a distinction must be drawn between decisions which can reasonably be made by individuals and decisions which require collective involvement. In practice it requires managers to be able to distinguish between decisions within the context of policies already determined collectively and those where policy development is necessary. The matter is not entirely resolved by stating that committees are responsible for policy and individuals for management because the two frequently interact. The effective working of the democratic process depends on clear arrangements for management accountability. If a manager is under pressure to make a decision which goes beyond policy previously determined by the appropriate committee, he/she must understand how the process of accountability will be applied.

Difficulties are often caused by poor communication and the restricted availability of information. If information is available to all operating in a common policy context consensus is likely to be norm. If it is not, the explanation will usually be found in hidden agendas: individuals operating on behalf of a sectional interest, or trying to create a favourable impression with an eye on promotion. In other words, there is an absence of another factor essential to the democratic process: openness.

Within the overall context of separation of powers, democratic subsidiarity, and adherence to the principles of information sharing and openness, the more detailed procedures to promote and safeguard the democratic process must be left to each institution. Subsidiarity embraces students and members of the community, and must be supported by clear and agreed processes at all stages. Although pure democracy may be a worthy objective, its credibility in colleges will depend on adopting a realistic and practical approach. To lean on Robinson again:

> A realistic and practical approach to democracy must acknowledge and accommodate the necessity that decisions must be taken both by collective bodies and by individuals. This is evident when we attempt to reconcile an ideal of democracy, as we must, with the ideal of personal liberty. Few would doubt that in education there must be room for individual decision-making by teachers and students. If so, then there must be room also for decision-making by technicians, administrators and managers.

Professor Robinson's paper is a valuable guide because it reflects both a commitment to the principle of democracy and a recognition of the difficulties of its practice. Colleges committed to the democratic process will, however, recognise what he calls its essence.

> Perhaps the essence of democracy is in the creation of a climate of democracy in which the normal expectation is that decisions will have *legitimacy* in that they are generally known and have consensual support. The decisions are legitimate in the sense that they are generally believed to have been made in a proper manner and from this they derive their authority. In a sense a democracy is satisfactory if the people involved have democratic expectations - that is to say expectations that everyone's views and needs are taken into account - and feel that these are being satisfactorily met. In this there is an element of circularity, of subjectivism - democracy is what people believe it to be and some communities may be satisfied in a way that others are not. The danger in this is of complacent submission to benevolent authoritarianism of those in powerful positions, the best safeguard against which is that those in key positions are pro-active practitioners of the democracy - not as a means of preserving their positions but as the means of advancing the collectively agreed objectives.

Applying the principle of democratic subsidiarity to the further education system in the UK requires legislation to define powers at three levels : national, regional, local (college). Associated with the powers given to college governors there must be a framework for further subsidiarity, indicating the powers of the academic board, the chief executive and senior managers, staff, students. Because democratic control also requires a participative approach to management, teaching and learning, curriculum development, colleges cannot function democratically without management and staff re-training on a large scale.

The concept of the Consortium, with the Revans' approach to management described in Chapter Five, is the model already at Bilston and under consideration in negotiations with CCASA. It is also a contribution to ongoing discussions with USA colleagues, where the focus is on how the community college concept must evolve as it is applied across the world. The Bilston model is not offered as *the* democratic solution but as *a* democratic solution, evolved to meet the challenges facing a particular college. Democracy, community education, the Revans' approach to management, all recognise that solutions cannot be imposed from outside: they must be allowed to evolve from the positive participation of all belonging to the organisation.

In accord with the same principle, *Further Education and Democracy* does not contain the appropriate response to all the challenges facing further education in the UK, or community colleges elsewhere in the world. Its contention is that, because it states a position resulting from democratic participation of students, staff, members of communities, all operating in an area of high unemployment and poverty, it should not be excluded from the debate. Colleges operating in partnerships with their communities have a contribution to make at least as valid and valuable as that of traditional universities and colleges.

It is the habit of vested interests to defend their position by disguising the issues.   In this case the choice for policy-makers is simple: between a meritocracy which rations education and training and a system open to all. The existing quangocracy in the UK, and the similar systems in other West European nations, have resulted in exclusions on a large scale: a democratic community college system aims to provide education and training for all.

The choice is quangocracy and exclusion, or democracy and inclusion.

Abbreviations and Acronyms

AACC	American Association of Community Colleges
ACIIE	American Council on International Intercultural Education
ACFHE	Association for Colleges of Further and Higher Education
ACPO	Association of Chief Police Officers
AfC	Association for Colleges
ALBSU	Adult Literacy and Basic Skills Unit
ANC	African National Congress
APC	Association of Principals of Colleges
APEL	Accreditation of Prior Experiential Learning
BSA	Basic Skills Agency
CCASA	Community Colleges Association of South Africa
CEF	Colleges' Employers' Forum
CSE	Certificate of Secondary Education
DE	Department of Employment
DES	Department of Education and Science
DfE	Department for Education
DfEE	Department for Education and Employment
DLE	Demand Led Element
EO & C	Equal Opportunities and Conferences
ESF	European Social Fund
FE	Further Education
FECG	Further Education Campaign Group
FEFC	Further Education Funding Council
FESR	Further Education Statistical Return
GCE	General Certificate of Education
GCSE	General Certificate of Secondary Education
GNVQ	General National Vocational Qualifications
HE	Higher Education
HMSO	Her Majesty's Stationery Office
IAETW	International Association for Education, Training and Work
LEA	Local Education Authority
MSC	Manpower Services Commission

NACETT	National Advisory Council for Education and Training Targets
NATFHE	National Association of Teachers in Further and Higher Education
NCVQ	National Council for Vocational Qualifications
NTET	National Targets for Education and Training
NVQ	National Vocational Qualifications
OCN	Open College Network
ODA	Overseas Development Administration
OECD	Organisation for Economic Co-operation and Development
PFI	Private Finance Initiative
QUANGO	Quasi-autonomous non-governmental organisation
SCAA	School Curriculum and Assessment Authority
SO	Scottish Office
TCA	Tertiary Colleges' Association
TEC	Training and Enterprise Council
TEED	Training, Enterprise and Education Directorate
TSA	Training Services Agency
UK	United Kingdom
USA	United States of America
WO	Welsh Office
YTS	Youth Training Schemes

References and bibliography

Basic Skills Agency. (1995), *Making an Impact: ALBSU's Annual Report 1993/94*, Basic Skills Agency.

Bilston Community College. (1996), *Basic Skills - An Assessment of Need in the Borough of Wolverhampton*, Bilston, Bilston Community College.

Black Country Careers Service Ltd. (BCCS) (1996), *1995 Destinations*, BCCS Ltd.

Caudwell, C. (1938), *Studies in a Dying Culture*, London, The Bodley Head.

Dearing, R. (1996), *Review of Qualifications for 16 - 19 Year Olds*, Hayes, SCAA.

Department of Education and Science. (1970), *Circular 7/70*, DES.

Department of Education and Science, Department of Employment, and Welsh Office. (1991), *Education and Training for the Twenty-first Century*, Vols 1 & 2 (Comnd 1536, May 1991), London, HMSO

Department for Education and Employment. Scottish Office, Wesh Office. (1995), *Lifetime Learning*: a consultation document. DfE, SO, WO.

Employment Department and Department for Education. (1995), *Competitiveness Forging Ahead* (Command 1867), London, ED and DfE.

Flint, C. and Austin, M (eds). (1994), *Going Further*, Bristol, Staff College.

HMSO. (1944), *Education Act, 1944*, London, HMSO.

HMSO. (1964), *Day Release: the report of the committee set up by the Minister of Education*, London, HMSO.

HMSO. (1964), *Industrial Training Act, 1964*, London, HMSO.

HMSO. (1988), *Education Reform Act, 1988*, London, HMSO.

HMSO. (1992), *European Communities Act, 1992*, London, HMSO.

HMSO. (1992), *Further and Higher Education Act, 1992*, London, HMSO.

HMSO. (1992), *The Education (Government of Further Education Corporations) (Former Further Education Colleges) Regulations 1992*, London, HMSO.

HMSO. (1994), *Competitiveness: Helping Business to Win*, London, HMSO.

HMSO. (1996) *Competitiveness: Creating the Enterprise Centre of Europe*, London, HMSO.

Home Office. (1995), *Young People and Crime* (Research Study 145), London, Home Office.

Hyams, E. (1963) *New Statesmanship: An Anthology*, London, Longmans.

International Institute for Management Development (1996), *World Competitiveness Yearbook 1996*, International Institute for Management Development.

National Advisory Council for Education and Training Targets. (1996) *Skills for 2000*, London, National Advisory Council for Education and Training Targets.

Reeves, F. (1995), *The Modernity of Further Education*, Wolverhampton, Bilston College, Education Now.

Robeson, P. (1963), *"Primitives"* in Hyams, op cit.

Robinson, E.E. (1968), *The New Polytechnics*, Harmondsworth, Penguin.

Robinson, E.E. (1990), *Democracy and Education*, Unpublished paper.

Shattock, M. (1994), *Derby College, Wilmorton: report on an enquiry into the governance and management of the college*, FEFC.

The Joseph Rowntree Trust. (1996), *The Future of Work*, The Joseph Rowntree Trust.

The Labour Party. (1996), *New Deal for a Lost Generation*, London, The Labour Party.

Tawney, R.H. (1964), *The Radical Tradition*, London, Pelican.

Training and Enterprise Councils' National Council. (1996), *Disaffection and non-participation in education, training and employment by individuals aged 18 - 20*, Sheffield, Aspire Consultants.

Wilkinson, C. (1995), *The Drop out Society*, Leicester, National Youth Agency.

Wymer, K. (1988), *Bilston College and Its Community*, Wolverhampton, Bilston Community College.

Wymer, K. (1994), *"Equal Opportunities and Further Education"* in Flint and Austin, op cit.

Index

Accreditation of Prior
Experiential Learning (APEL), 51.
ADAPT, 83, 84.
additionality, 31.
adult education, 2, 6-8, 15, 17, 31, 38,
39, 44,59, 76, 97, 99.
ALBSU, 42, 45.
African Cultural Centre, 78.
African National Congress, 76, 105.
All Party Committee for Tertiary
Education, 4.
All Party Committee of the House
of Commons, 4.
American Association of
Community Colleges, 81, 86-87.
American Council on
International Intercultural Education,
81, 85, 86, 106.
Association for Colleges (AfC), 4, 84.
Association of Colleges for
Further and Higher Education, 3, 4, 17.
Association of Principals of Colleges, 3,
4, 17, 36.

basic skills, 10, 26, 30, 41-42, 45-46, 50,
54, 78, 95, 97.
Bilston Community College (BCC), 7, 39,
42, 55, 56, 61-62, 64, 68-69, 71, 78, 89.
Bilston Community College Foundation,
71.
BCC companies:
Bilston (E.O.& C.) Training Ltd, 64,
69, 71.
Stowlawn Ltd, 64, 66, 69, 71, 73, 78.

Bilston Consortium, 59, 68, 70-71,
76, 80-81, 85, 87, 105.
Bilston Friends of Open Education,
61-62, 65.
Bird, J., 62.
Black Country Partnership College,
71.
Blunkett, D., 3.
Boswell, T., 2.
Bovis, J., 4.
British College of Banking and
Finance (Moscow), 75, 78, 80, 81.
British Steel, 61-62.
Brown, G., 3.

Carver, G., 62.
Chadwell Securities Ltd, 81.
Charity Know How, 80.
Clarke, K., 1, 2, 15.
Colleges' Employers Forum, 2, 22.
Collingwood, J., 62.
Community Colleges Association of
South Africa (CCASA), 76, 85,
105-106, 109.
Community Colleges, 7, 38-41,
49-50, 55, 59-60, 68, 72-73, 75-76,
78, 81, 85-89, 94, 97, 100, 104-106,
109-110.
community:
education, 7, 15, 31, 37, 41-42, 44,
46-47, 49-55, 57, 59-60, 62,
65-66, 68, 71, 77, 87, 109.
programmes, 60.
regeneration, 51.
competency-based qualifications, 20.

comprehensive schools, 9, 41.
Confederation of British Industries, 96.
convergence (funding), 56.
County Colleges, 8, 38.
CSE, 9.

Davies, B., 3.
day release, 3, 8-10, 14, 40, 47, 101.
Dearing, R., 96-97:
Committee, 96-97, 105.
Report, 39, 42, 94-95, 100.
Demand Led Element (DLE), 54-55.
Department for Education, 3, 6, 19, 22-24, 27, 46, 50, 53.
Department for Education and Employment, 6, 19, 24, 30, 46, 50, 53, 94-95, 99.
Department of Education and Science, 8, 17, 30.
Department of Employment, 1, 3, 8, 10, 14-15, 17, 19, 25, 40-41, 46, 60, 91, 95.
Department of Science and Arts, 38.
Derby Tertiary College (Wilmorton), 22-24, 27-28, 55.

Eastern Europe, 69, 72, 81.
economic regeneration, 7, 77, 90-91, 94, 99, 101-102.
Education Act (1918), 50.
Education Act (1944), 8, 38, 50.
Education Reform Act (1988), 8, 12-13, 24, 26, 28, 57, 63, 98.
Edwards, B., 61-62, 82.
Elsner, P., 81.
employers, 1-2, 4, 8-12, 15-17, 20, 24-26, 38-39, 41, 46, 54, 60, 64, 70, 72-73, 83-85, 97, 100-101.

equal opportunities, 7, 14, 31, 46, 49, 53-58, 62, 64, 69, 77, 82, 96,101.
European Communities Act (1992), 83, 90.
European Commission, 1, 31, 34, 43, 68, 81, 83-84.
European Parliament, 62, 81, 84.
European Union, 51, 76, 83-85, 90-91.
European Social Fund, 10, 31, 40, 56, 63.
European Year of Lifelong Learning, 46, 50-51, 94:
exclusion, 43-44, 49-51, 55, 110.

Fatchett, D., 3.
Federation of British Industries, 45.
Forman, N., 2.
Flower, F., 8.
full-time education, 9-10, 14, 25, 39, 40, 101.
Funda Centre, 78.
funding, 1-6, 9-11, 14, 17-20, 23, 27 30-33, 36, 39, 41, 44, 49-50, 52-58, 62-63, 65, 68, 70-73, 75, 78, 81, 83-84, 92, 94, 97, 101, 106.
Further and Higher Education Act (1992), 2-3, 5-6, 14-15, 17-20, 29, 31, 41-42, 44, 48-50, 53, 55, 76, 94.
Further Education Campaign Group, 3, 4, 17.
FE colleges, 1-2, 8-9, 15-16, 27, 32, 39, 41, 45, 59-60, 102.
Further Education Funding Council (FEFC), 4-7, 15, 17-24, 27-33, 36-37, 39, 49-50, 52-58, 63, 65-69, 71-72, 79, 84, 98, 106.

118

Further Education Staff College, 60.
further educational statistical return
(FESR), 10.
GCE A level, 9-10, 14, 25, 40, 42, 44,
47-48, 52, 61, 94-95, 100.
GCE O level, 9, 44.
GCSE, 44.

Handsworth College, 54-55.
Hargreaves, K., 4.
Haynes, A., 62.
higher education, 2-6, 15, 17-20, 29, 31,
38, 41-42, 44, 47, 52, 54, 76.
Hill, C., 45.

Industrial Training Act (1964), 8, 10, 25,
38.
Industrial Training Boards, 8, 10, 16, 25,
38.
International Association for Education
Training and Work, 85, 89.
International Institute for Management
Development, 95.

Job Training Scheme, 44.
Joseph Rowntree Foundation, 50.

Kyte, J., 62.

Labour Party, 2, 3, 90-91, 94, 99-101.
Lamb, H., 8.
Leicestershire Community College, 59.
LEONARDO, 83.
Liberal democrats, 6.
lifelong learning, 16, 31, 46, 49-51, 78.

Maheney, J., 81.
Major, J., 2, 50.

Makhene, M., 106.
Manpower Services Commission
(MSC), 11, 16, 18, 25, 38, 40, 44,
94.
Maricopa Community College, 81.
McClure, 5.
meritocracy, 38, 44, 53, 104, 110.
Millington, A., 62, 105.
Ministry of Education, 8.
Molatoli, D., 106.
Montserrat project, 78, 81, 89.
Mould, G., 62.
Mulcahy, M., 106.
Murphy, S., 62.

National Association of Teachers in
Further and Higher Education
(NATFHE), 4-5, 35.
National Council for Vocational
Qualifications (NCVQ), 20, 94.
National Institute of Community
Education (NICE), 105.
National Advisory Council for
Education and Training Targets
(NACETT), 99.
National Targets for Educational
Training (NTET), 1, 19, 21, 46,
52-53, 94.
National Vocational Qualifications
(NVQ), 14, 18, 52.
National Youth Agency, 42.
non-vocational education, 3, 14, 25,
31.

Oil and Gas Corporation, 78.
Open College of the Black Country,
72.
Open College Network, 15, 18, 30, 52.

Organisation for Economic Co-operation and Development (OECD), 52.
outreach, 54-55, 75, 80.
Overseas Development Administration, 1, 79.

Partridge, E., 81.
part-time education, 8, 39-40.
Patten, J., 1-2, 6, 21.
Pierce, D., 81.
Pitt, T., 62.
polytechnics, 15, 38, 46, 52, 54.
post-16 education, 7, 9, 13, 18, 94, 99, 105.
Private Finance Initiative, 21.
public schools, 17, 38.
quangocracy, 5, 18, 23, 27, 49, 53, 58, 83, 100, 106.
quangos, 11, 14, 18, 20, 23-24, 26-27, 32, 36-38, 58, 68, 92-94.
Revans, R., 75, 109;
action learning, 75.
Robinson, E., 7, 46, 106-108.
Rooker, J., 96.

Semoon Ltd, 69, 71.
Shattock, M., 23.
Shattock Report, 23.
Single Regeneration Budget, 84, 101.
sixth form colleges, 1, 4, 6, 9, 17, 19, 39.
Sixth Form Colleges' Association, 4, 17.
Social Chapter, 83.
South Africa, 49, 69, 72-73, 75-78, 81-82, 85-87, 105.
special educational needs, 12, 25, 53, 57.
Springvale Co-operative, 62, 65, 69, 71, 73.
Springvale Training Ltd, 69.

Straw, J., 2, 3.
Stubbs, B., 5.
Student Centred Learning, 48.

Tawney, R. H., 45-46, 62.
Technical colleges, 39, 60, 105.
technology, 51, 75, 78, 82-83, 87-88.
TEC National Council (1996), 42, 96.
Tertiary colleges, 3-4, 9, 17, 19, 39.
Tertiary Colleges' Association, 3-4, 17.
Thatcher, M., 27.
Thompson, E. P., 45.
Trade Unions, 2, 9, 13, 35, 41, 45, 61-62, 85.
Training and Enterprise Councils (TECs), 3, 6, 17, 19-20, 39, 101.
Training Services Agency, 39.
Turner, D., 4, 62, 105.

United Kingdom, 1, 6, 38, 41-43, 45-47, 49-52, 68, 76-78, 84, 86, 90, 92, 95, 100-101, 106, 109.
United States of America, 7, 39-40, 45, 50, 57, 60, 63, 75-76, 81, 85-87, 89, 106, 109.
universities, 1-2, 17, 38, 40, 44, 46, 48, 52, 83, 94, 96-98, 101-102, 105, 110.
University of Wolverhampton, 78, 81, 89.

Van Trease, D., 81.
Venton, F., 62.
vocationalism, 6, 11, 15, 18, 20, 31, 40-41, 43, 45-46, 50-52, 69, 85, 95, 97, 105.

Ward, R., 4.
Western Europe, 78, 83.
White papers:
  Competitiveness, 46, 50, 97.
  Forging Ahead, 6, 19, 21, 97.
  Education and Training, 1, 3, 14, 49.
  Training and Learning, 43, 51, 91.
  Youth Opportunities, 8.
Williams, R., 45.

Young, D., 27.
Youth Training Schemes, 26, 42, 60,
  95, 100.

Zuma, S., 105.